All About the Flowering World

allabout
books

All About
the Flowering
World

By Ferdinand C. Lane

Illustrated by Russell Francis Peterson

RANDOM HOUSE
NEW YORK

All About the Flowering World

Iris

Sweetpea

Peony

Contents

Rue
anemone

Trilium

Jack-in-the-
pulpit

Violet

1.

A Close-up of the Flower

We live in a world of flowers. They sprinkle the meadows with buttercups and daisies. They make tropic forests flame with color. Arctic explorers find them along the edges of melting ice. Camel drivers in the desert see them beside sun-baked rocks and sand. Farmers are glad to have them on growing beans and squashes and tomatoes. Florists experiment for years on blossoms of strange form or color. And wherever they bloom, they add beauty to this world of ours.

What thrilling tales they could tell us—tales filled with more action than hunting lions, more adventures than Robinson Crusoe ever knew! Even the tiniest blossom is making a brave struggle to live in an unfriendly world of storm and drought and countless enemies. It has a story to tell us that goes back long ages to a time when the world was young and life first began. We can read that story in the fossils of ancient rocks. It is repeated every spring when apple trees are in bud and southern fields glow with cotton blooms. For it is the very story of creation that is still going on everywhere.

These flowering plants mean a great deal to us. They purify the air we breathe. They protect our hillsides from crumbling in the rains. They give us shelter and clothing and fuel to keep us warm and cook our meals. They manufacture food for all living things. For only plants can take the dead elements from earth and air and water and rearrange them in the sugar and starch and protein and fat that feed the world. Plants are the source of all other life, and without them no life could long survive.

Iris

Sweetpea

Peony

There are flowers of many sizes and shapes.

All Shapes, Sizes and Colors

Even the humblest blossom is really a tiny workshop where things are being done that no chemist can equal. In his laboratory a chemist can change one substance into others. He is even learning how to tear apart the atoms that make up all matter. But he cannot awake in matter that mysterious thing that we call life.

Yet the flower performs this miracle. And when its brief day is ended and it fades and withers, it leaves behind the beginning of a new life which we call a seed.

If we look at flowers closely, we can learn something of the secrets they can tell us from their shape and sizes and colors. How many kinds there are, and how different! What a variety of shapes! Some are almost flat like

3

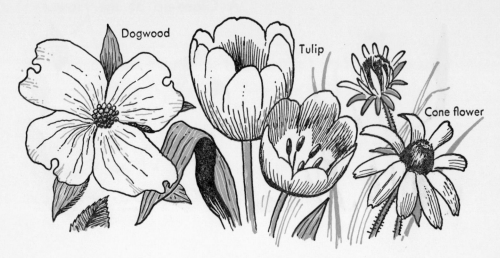

The dogwood is almost flat while the tulip is cup-shaped.

the pansy or dogwood blossom. Some are cup-shaped like the tulip. Some resemble tiny horns like the blossoms of the trumpet vine. Some, the fuchsias and columbines, hang downward like little Japanese lanterns. Some unfold in fluffy masses like the peony, or are feathery like the chrysanthemum, or fluted like the carnation. And some have strange shapes like the orchid or the snapdragon.

In size they differ even more. Blossoms of the grass are so tiny that we seldom see them. Those of the magnolia or giant water lily may be a foot across. A few tropic species are even larger. Flowers may grow singly like the dandelion or daisy, or in masses like the lilac or hydrangea. Banana blossoms form in spirals about a big

4

central bud. The Talipot palm sends up a stalk that may be thirty feet high and may comprise as many as sixty million blossoms!

And flowers have more colors than the rainbow. But every detail of size and shape and color is designed for one purpose only. And that purpose is to help the flower develop seed.

How a Flower Is Put Together

Flowers reveal simply and beautifully the story of reproduction.

We can get the picture more clearly by dissecting a simple blossom which will serve as a type for all the rest. About this blossom, as it opened, an outer covering formed as a protection. This is called the *calyx* from the Greek word meaning cup, which it resembles. The separate leaves of the calyx are called *sepals*. The body of the flower within the calyx is known as the *corolla* and its leaves are the *petals* which are often bright colored and sweet scented. In the center of the corolla is a stalk called the *pistil*. Often it is shaped like a tiny water bottle. The upper tip is the *stigma*, the narrow neck the *style*, and the bulging lower part the *ovary*. This in turn

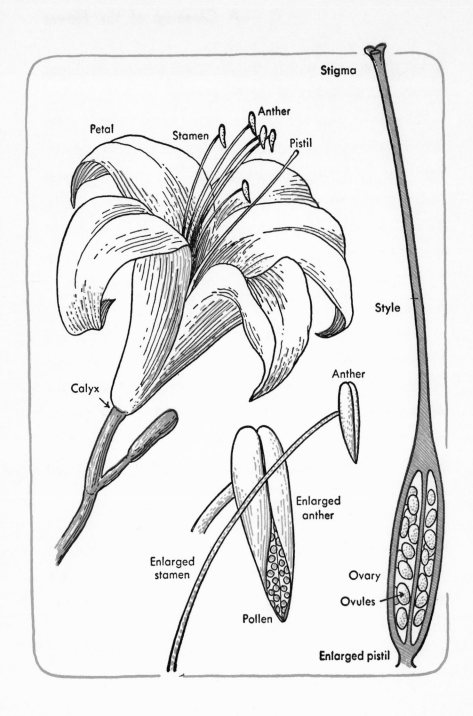

Stigma

Anther

Petal   Stamen   Pistil

Calyx

Anther

Enlarged
anther

Enlarged
stamen

Pollen

Style

Ovary

Ovules

Enlarged pistil

holds the *ovules* which may develop into seeds. These are the female parts of the flower.

About the pistil are grouped other more slender stalks called *stamens*. Each stamen comprises a filament bearing at its tip a tiny case, an *anther*. The anther contains many grains of *pollen* which are the germs of life. When one grain of pollen touches a stigma, it works its way into the ovary where it unites with an ovule to form a seed. Stamens and anthers are the male parts of the flower.

In such a flower, both sexes are combined in a single blossom. Although this is a common arrangement, the ovules and pollen grains seldom mature at the same time. Seeds are usually formed by union with pollen from another flower. Many flowers are purely feminine and are called *pistillate;* others purely masculine, are called *staminate*.

Some blossoms are far more complex than this. In these, the pistil may comprise several *carpels*, each one containing its own stigma, style and ovary. At the same time there may be hundreds of stamens, each bearing an anther filled with pollen grains. But whatever the pattern, it serves a single purpose. And that purpose is to kindle a spark of life within an ovule by uniting with a pollen grain so that a seed may form and a new plant may bloom.

Because plants can reproduce, they have multiplied in almost every part of the world.

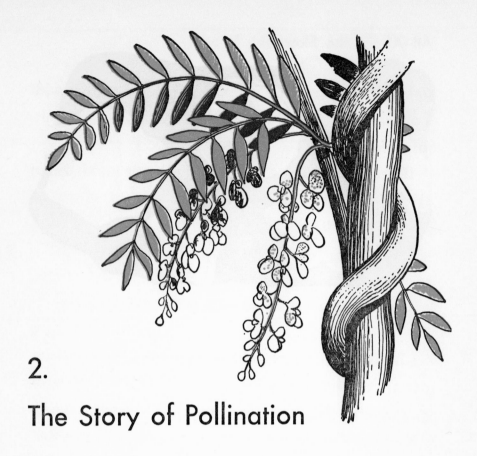

2.

The Story of Pollination

Dust Finer Than Gold

All about us there is a dust more valuable than all the gold in the world. That dust is pollen.

Pollen grains are very small. They range from 1/300 to 1/700 of an inch in length. In shape they usually resemble tiny grains of wheat or rice. But if we peer through a microscope, we shall find stranger forms. For some are three-cornered, some cylindrical, some like little golf balls, and some like the crescent moon.

Under a microscope we see pollen grains of many shapes.

Chemists tell us that pollen grains are made of protoplasm, the basic substance of all living things. With it are mingled oily particles and sometimes starch. Usually a grain contains two cells. One of these divides into two other cells called *gametes*. A gamete combines with an ovule to form a seed. This is called *fertilization*.

After a pollen grain has touched the stigma, the time needed to fertilize a flower varies greatly. In dandelions and lettuce a few minutes are enough. In oaks and alders a full year may be required. The usual time ranges from twenty-four to forty-eight hours.

A few flowering plants that bear both pistils and stamens pollinate themselves. This is true of peas and tomatoes and cereal grains. But most plants get pollen from another blossom, often from another plant. Pollen grains are so fine that they can be blown about by the wind. Actually this is very wasteful, for billions of grains are lost while one is finding the right blossom. In pine woods we often find golden pollen covering everything and even collecting in windrows.

Some of the peat used in Europe as fuel is made up mostly of pollen grains that have collected for thousands of years. But pollen has left traces far older than in peat. For fossil samples have been found in rocks of the Jurassic Period, 150 million years ago.

Help From Insects and Birds

The winds scatter pollen among poplar trees and grasses. Even water floats the tiny grains to plants that bloom in ponds and marshes. But most blossoms must depend upon some bird or insect for this necessary work. So a friendly partnership has grown up between the animal kingdom and the flowering world.

The age of the great awkward dinosaurs that once roamed the earth ended long ago, and with it went giant tree ferns and club mosses and other strange vegetation. Then all the world burst into bloom with thousands of species of plants where only a few had grown before. Animal life multiplied as well. At last the uplands were bright with flowers and musical with the hum of insects and the song of birds.

Meanwhile, each blossom developed distinctive color, size and shape to attract some animal helper to distribute its pollen. In return, the flower offered such delicacies as pollen and nectar.

Just as some birds and insects love sweet nectar, so bees love pollen. They collect it on their legs and bear it homeward to the hive to make into bee bread. This has a bitter taste, but bees value it as food even more than honey. Some flowers, like the poppy and rock rose, produce pollen but no nectar.

Watch a bee as it visits one blossom after another. It forces its way into the flower for nectar. When it comes out, its body is dusted with yellow pollen. Then it buzzes to another blossom where some of the pollen from the first flower is rubbed off. The pollen touches the stigma and works its way into the ovary where the ovules are hidden that turn into seeds.

Many flowers of the temperate zone, particularly in dry regions, attract bees. Among the bees' favorite flowers are snapdragon, mint, orange blossoms and blossoms of the plane tree. Perhaps the favorite is white clover.

Stigma

Pistil

Anther

Petal

A bee may carry pollen from the anther of one flower to the
stigma of another.

All About the Flowering World

Red clover is too big a problem for the honeybee. The nectar lies so deep her short tongue cannot reach it. But her cousin, the bumblebee, can. Bumblebees press their weight into the clover bloom and with their longer tongues lap up the nectar. As they come away, the pollen clings to their bodies. Then they visit other blossoms and dust off some of the golden particles. When red clover was introduced into Australia, it would not grow until bumblebees were brought in to carry pollen from one blossom to another.

But while bees are the most useful insects in scattering pollen, they have many rivals. When figs were brought to California, they grew well but did not produce good fruit. And it was not until a wasp was brought over from the Near East that figs could be grown for market. For like bees, this wasp helps to carry pollen from one flower to another and thus fertilize the figs. Butterflies flit about on the same errand, but they are fragile and short-lived. Moths which are more active work mostly at night. They are fond of tobacco blossoms, the evening primrose, and the night-blooming cereus. The yucca cannot develop seeds unless one particular species of moth is on hand to gather pollen and deposit it in the stigma chamber of the flower.

Some flies also serve the flowers. They are most active in mountain regions or those which border the Arctic. But they also carry pollen to buttercups, trilliums and Dutchman's-breeches.

A few of the beetles are expert gardeners. They pollinate the blossoms of the magnolia, the wild rose and the water lily. And there are other insect helpers, including even ants.

Some birds like nectar, particularly hummingbirds. In seeking such sweets, they also pollinate the blossoms. Among their favorites are honeysuckle, fuchsias and

Hummingbirds, seeking nectar, also pollinate the blossoms.

columbines. Banana blossoms attract them, and they seem to be the only creature that fertilizes pineapples.

Still higher in the scale of life are bats, for they are mammals. They, too, labor among the blossoms of curious plants like the areca palm and the sausage tree.

By this time, man has learned that he must help in pollinating flowers if he wants the best results. In our apple orchards we often set up beehives to make sure that pollen carriers are on hand to do their work. And in California, date growers have learned that the date palm will not produce good fruit unless a strand of male blossoms is inserted among female flowers. So forty-nine female trees are planted around one male tree. Thus the pollen from a single plant helps produce fine crops of dates on forty-nine others.

Why Flowers Have Nectar

Nectar is mostly water. Its sugar content varies with the blossom and even the time of day. Showers dilute it and reduce its sweetness. Yet it may be one-third sugar with traces of other foods, such as carbohydrates and proteins, to give it flavor.

Nectar forms in tiny sacs called nectary glands, often

From many kinds of flowers bees gather nectar to make honey.

buried among the petals. Bees must burrow for this nectar which they use in making honey.

The nectar they swallow goes into "honey sacs" inside their bodies. There it undergoes certain changes. In the hive it is poured into little boxlike cells called honeycomb which the bees have made from wax. But their work is not yet finished. They gather about these cells and vibrate their wings at a rate of 400 times a second until more water is evaporated and the nectar becomes honey. Eighty thousand field trips may be needed for one pound of honey. And those field trips, if stretched end to end, would take a honeybee twice around the globe.

But bees do even more for us. For they select special kinds of nectar to make different brands of honey. When they find the flower they like best, they will gather nectar from no other. And so we have honey flavored from white clover, from buckwheat, from orange blossoms and many others. The tiny pink blooms of the cranberry yield honey with a slightly sour flavor.

Many plants also secrete nectar on leaves and stems outside the blossoms. There it attracts ants which may distribute pollen. These ants are even more useful as tiny watchdogs to protect the plant from insect enemies. In Mediterranean countries, ants are encouraged to build nests about the trunks of fruit trees because they devour certain pests which would otherwise attack the fruit or leaves. This is another example of the friendly partnership between the animal kingdom and the flowering world.

Fragrance for a Purpose

When we speak of sweetness in flowers, we mean their fragrance rather than their nectar. Fragrance is also

Flowers attract birds and insects with their fragrance.

secreted by tiny sacs among the petals or the surrounding leaves. Flowers have fragrance for just one purpose —to attract birds and insects which will carry pollen.

Bees will fly straight to a honeysuckle vine several hundred yards away even though they cannot see it. The odor and their keen sense of smell have guided them.

This odor may be faint as in the lily of the valley, or strong as in the narcissus. In Florida the scent of night-blooming jasmine is almost overpowering.

The fragrance of orange groves or apple orchards in blossom carries far. Explorers among the Spice Islands could smell the clove trees before they appeared above the misty horizon.

But flowers are fragile things. So plant odors may linger in the leaves, the fruit, the seeds, the bark, and even in the wood. Seeds may be strongly scented as in caraway and celery seeds that we use for flavoring. The bark may be fragrant as in cinnamon. Even the wood itself may have a sweet aroma as do sandalwood and cedar.

On a hot day the smell of pines is quite as pleasing as their shade. New-mown hay and sweet grasses have a special fragrance of their own. We use mint leaves to add flavor to our foods and the leaves of herbs to season certain dishes. To a cat the fragrance of the catnip leaf is almost intoxicating.

In India, more than most countries, the fragrance of flowers has been esteemed. Some of the early emperors arranged their gardens so that not only the color of the blossoms but their fragrance would make pleasing combinations.

But the sweetness which blossoms distill fades when they die. And so, for ages, men have tried to preserve that sweetness. In olden days petals were collected in "rose jars" with tightly fitting tops. By removing the cover, one could smell the fragrance of hundreds of flowers that had bloomed many years before.

Perfume has long been extracted from blossoms. In France its manufacture is an important industry. The process is delicate, for the scent is easily lost. Millions of pounds of roses, orange blossoms, and other flowers are gathered. Many things affect their fragrance—moisture in the air, the time of day, the maturity of the blossom.

Many materials have been used in the attempt to "fix" perfumes. One of the best is a strange, waxy substance called ambergris found in the bodies of sperm whales. At times lumps of it even wash ashore and have brought several hundred dollars a pound.

In Bulgaria large areas are devoted to growing roses. From their petals an oil is distilled called attar of roses, the basis of a sweet perfume. Thirty blossoms yield only one drop of this oil, and 32,000 are required for a pound.

Not all flowers are fragrant, however. Some have little or no odor. Others, like the marigold and the geranium, have strong scents that some people dislike. And there are blossoms we would not care to have around. One of these is a glossy green plant of early spring, well-named skunk cabbage. In the tropics we might find even worse offenders—colorful flowers that smell like decaying fish. But they serve the same useful purpose as sweeter odors. For they attract flies that spread their pollen to other blossoms.

A Rainbow of Colors

It is not fragrance, however, that we most admire in flowers. It is their color. And the real purpose of color is to attract some bird or insect which will distribute pollen.

Blossoms which are pollinated by the winds do not need such help. So they are small and seldom seen. The grasses and the grains are among these.

But most flowers make a bright display to attract the creatures which will spread their pollen. Flowering trees, such as the flamboyant, can be seen for miles as though the tropic forest were on fire. And smaller plants do quite as well in a more limited range.

Of course, neither birds nor insects come to admire their colors. They are looking for something to eat— nectar or pollen—and the colors are like waving flags that invite them to the feast. Just as color attracts insects

The glossy green skunk cabbage appears in early spring.

to flower masses, so fragrance guides them to a particular blossom. But some blossoms, pansies for example, go even further. For they have markings on their petals which direct insects to the hidden nectar.

Markings on pansy petals guide insects to hidden nectar.

Bees are attracted long distances by red, pink or blue blossoms. They do not see white or yellow colors from such distances. But near at hand they investigate them also. Pale shades of pink and purple seem to lure moths and butterflies.

As they grow older, flowers change color. White blossoms turn pink, then tan or even brown before they die.

Like the blossoms, the leaves, stems, and roots often have a vivid color. While most leaves are green, they may contain other dyes. One of these is a bright red that we find in the petals of a canna and the skin of a radish. Another is an orange yellow common both in flowers and carrots. In northern states, when the green fades from the leaves in autumn, other dyes appear, such as yellow, orange and flame red. Then birch and maple and scarlet oak make hillsides glow with brilliant color.

Many flowering plants produce useful dyes. American Indians used the juices of roots and berries to dye their wool.

For centuries saffron has been an important dye. It is made from the dried stigmas of flowers that flourish in the beautiful Vale of Kashmir in northern India. The blossoms are purple, but the stigmas are a rich yellow. Saffron was imported by the Greeks and Romans. For it also gave them a sweet perfume. Raising saffron is still an important industry. For no fewer than 75,000 blossoms are needed for a single pound of saffron.

Another plant that also yields sweet scents as well as

color is lavender. Still more important is the indigo, a plant native to India. When it reaches a height of four to six feet, it is cut down and a rich, bluish-purple dye is obtained from the juices of its stalks.

Another dye comes from plants growing in Central America. An insect called the cochineal bug aids in the process. The juices which it sucks cover its body and when it dies yield a rich red. Insects also sting a species of oak that grows in the Near East so that hollow swellings form on the twigs. These are called "mad apples" and make a dye called "turkey red."

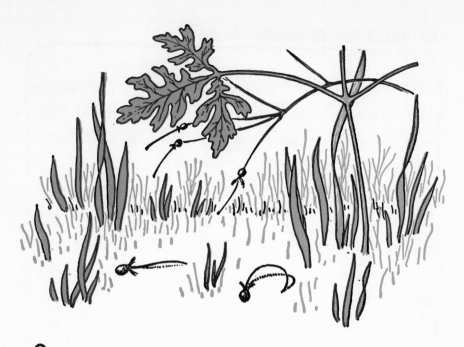

3.

Seeds and Their Ways

A Plant in a Package

A seed is really an unborn new plant in package form. It contains a tiny stem and root and leaves all ready to grow. It also holds food enough to nourish the baby plant until it can feed itself with substances it gets from soil and air and water under the warm sunlight. These are all tightly wrapped as protection from rain and frost and other perils.

Seeds are of many shapes. Some, like turnip seeds, are

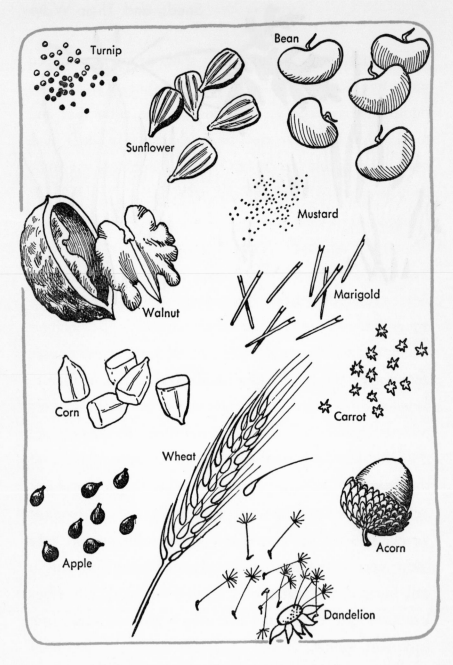

Seeds are of many shapes, sizes and colors.

tiny globes that look like bird shot. Many are shaped more like little footballs; others, the sunflower and the pumpkin, have flat seeds. Those of the cucumber and muskmelon look like tiny boats. Not a few seeds have queer curves and may even resemble corkscrews. Some have strange hooks and horns and tails.

Seeds are of many colors. Black and white, gray and brown are common. Many seeds are red or orange or yellow. And not a few are striped.

In size seeds differ even more. Those of the poppy are as fine as dust. At the other extreme is the coconut which is one big seed. Largest of all is the great double coconut of the Seychelles Islands in the Indian Ocean. One of these huge seeds may weigh as much as forty pounds. Sailors who first found them floating at sea thought they had been spewed up by some monster of the deep.

Many seeds are so well protected they will live for years. Seeds of the wattle tree of Australia are so hard they must sometimes be boiled so that the life within can burst forth and grow. Even seeds with coverings less hard and tough may live a long time. Wheat from Egyptian tombs, several thousand years old, has been made into good bread. It is unlikely it would grow if planted. But wheat kept for thirty years has produced crops. For the life within the seed can sleep a long time before it wakes.

How Seeds Are Scattered

But it is not enough for plants to produce seeds. They must scatter them about. This problem has been solved in many ways.

In the western part of the United States we might meet a queer plant, dry and shriveled, bouncing along before the wind. It is called the tumbleweed. Its seeds can travel far because the plant scatters them as it tumbles along. Most plants cannot move, of course, so they must depend upon other means to scatter their seeds.

In tall trees this may be a simple matter. Acorns, dropping from a big oak, may go bounding away to some snug resting place.

But the winds are the great distributors. Seeds of the iris and the poppy are so fine they are scattered like dust. In some plants the seeds are fastened to tiny parachutes which the wind carries along. Seeds of the dandelion, breaking loose, drift over broad pasture lands.

The dried tumbleweed scatters its seeds as it rolls along.

So do the feathery tufts of the milkweed and the thistle. We do not commonly think of cotton plants in that class, but the soft fibers which we weave into cloth are designed solely to bear the seeds away on the wind. The huge kapok tree of the East Indies has similar seeds attached to fibers, sometimes called silk cotton.

Many trees have winged seeds that drift like tiny gliders. The ash grows seeds in "keys" or wings, each bearing a seed. Seeds of the maple are joined in pairs, their outspread wings resembling an airplane propeller. In the sycamore the wings are twisted to carry even farther.

Seeds of many plants such as lilies and begonias have paper-like borders and act like tiny kites. A few plants use the principle of the balloon to scatter seeds. The bladder-senna which flourishes inside the crater of Vesuvius grows its seeds in a swollen pod which dries and floats away through the air.

Ocean currents are great seed distributors. Coconuts have floated all over the Indian and Pacific oceans. After drifting for weeks or even months, they may wash ashore on some coral beach and, splitting open, send down roots and lift tall trunks so sturdy they defy even typhoons.

The seeds of the Indian mulberry are in a sort of bladder which can float long distances. Seeds of the Japanese black currant often wash ashore along the coast of Oregon, after floating across the widest of oceans. In fresh waters the seeds of the water lily have a spongy belt filled with air chambers like a life preserver. When this belt decays, the seeds sink to the bottom and take root. Seeds of the sedges are in little sacks which float

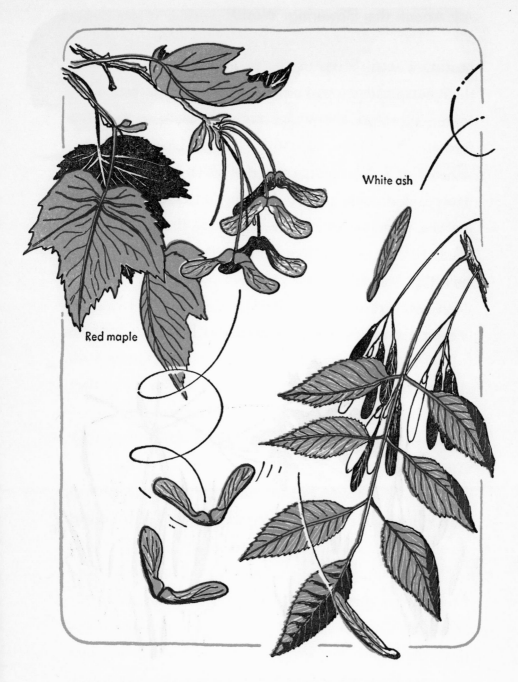

White ash

Red maple

Many trees have winged seeds that drift like tiny gliders.

about as though they were seeking some good home.

When the bean pod ripens, it dries and twists. Then some day it splits open and the beans are scattered. The broom plant, with its bright yellow blossoms, grows similar pods. The violet and the witch hazel have pods that explode when ripe, shooting out seeds as though from a popgun. The sandbox tree of the tropics has a seed pod which explodes with a report almost as loud as a pistol shot.

A few strange plants develop seeds that crawl about almost like insects. Such is the crane's bill, so called from

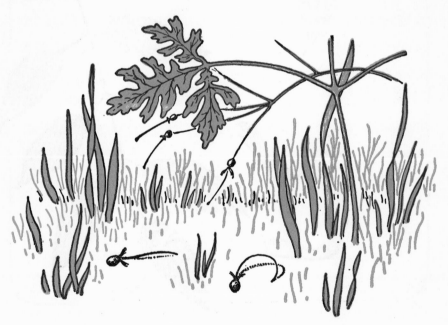

The seeds of the crane's bill wriggle along like insects.

the long beak upon its seed pod. Each seed inside has bristles and a long tail or awn. Upon the ground this awn curls like a corkscrew in dry weather and uncurls when damp. Such movements send the seed wriggling along until it finds the right spot where it drives its sharp point downward and the bristles hold it firmly. Some grass seeds have similar awns or tails.

Many plants depend upon some animal to scatter their seeds as well as their pollen. Birds are tireless planters of berries or small fruits. Squirrels not only scatter seeds but plant them also. They hide acorns and other nuts for winter food, but often forget some of them. And so, in future years, a big oak may grow from an acorn that a squirrel had buried and forgotten.

Some seeds have sharp hooks and barbs that cling to the wool or fur of animals and even our own clothes or stockings. Such are sticktights and Spanish mead and burdocks. In Chile a traveler observed wild horses with manes and tails so tangled with burs they could hardly walk.

A plant of evil reputation is the feather grass of Russia. The seed is fastened to a feather-like streamer that carries it before the wind. It also has a slender tail or awn like that of the crane's bill which unwinds when damp and drives into the ground where the barbs hold fast. But the seeds sometimes tangle in the wool of a sheep. They pierce the skin, burrowing ever deeper, tormenting and even killing the poor animal.

Plants still more dangerous are found in Africa. One of these has seed cases called "devil's horns." Grazing animals, antelopes or oxen, sometimes get these seed cases in their nostrils where they cling with their cruel hooks. Meanwhile, the poor animals rush frantically about, suffer greatly and may even die.

Still worse is the grapnel plant whose seed cases, which look something like a crab, have sharp claws an inch long. Even the lion may fall victim to this terrible weed. Rolling on the ground like a dog, he feels his skin pierced by the sharp claws. And when he tries to tear them out with his teeth, they get in his mouth and he may even die of starvation.

Fruits as Seed Covers

As seeds develop from the ovules inside the ovary, the ovary itself becomes a fruit. Sometimes this also includes the calyx which surrounds the blossom or even a bit of stalk. We think of fruits as pulpy like a peach,

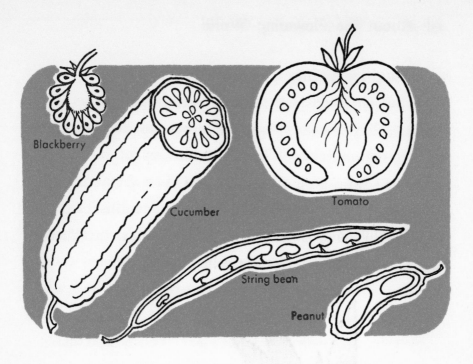

To a scientist all seed coverings are "fruits."

or juicy like an orange. We are doubtful about berries and so call them "small fruits." We argue about fruits and vegetables. We are quite sure string beans are vegetables, but what about tomatoes or muskmelons? And nuts, of course, are different, we say. But the scientist recognizes no such distinctions. To him cotton bolls, no less than bean pods or persimmons, are "fruits." For they, too, develop from the ovaries of blossoms when seeds are formed.

Most fruits, such as lemons or blueberries, come from a single ovary. But blossoms with several ovaries may combine a number of fruits in one. In the raspberry each tiny compartment is a separate fruit. Such fruits are called *aggregate*. And there are more complicated ones like the pineapple. Each section traced on its spiny skin developed from an individual flower. For the pineapple in bloom is a cluster of little blue blossoms that do not open at the same time, and the fruit builds up almost like a house. Such fruits are called *collective*.

Each section you see on a pineapple skin developed from a separate flower. In a raspberry each compartment is a fruit.

In the pear the pulpy flesh develops from the calyx of the flower and the part which supports the ovary. The ovary itself appears only in the inner chambers which hold the seeds. Such fruits are called *pomes*. Most fruits contain many seeds; others, like the cherry or the apricot, have only one. They are known as *drupes*.

Chestnuts are really seeds, but the spiny case which holds them is a fruit. Still better armored are Brazil nuts. Though each kernel has its own hard shell, the nuts, which may number twenty or more, are enclosed in a flinty case shaped something like a cannon ball. It is so hard we would need an ax to break it.

Whether the seed covering is pulpy flesh like a plum or a hard case like a Brazil nut, its purpose is to protect the seed inside. Scientists call such seeds "covered seeds" to distinguish them from others not so well protected.

Not So Well Protected

There are plants which produce seeds in more simple ways. Their blossoms are small and seldom seen. Their wind-blown pollen comes directly in contact with their ovules. And no true fruits develop to cover them. So they are called *naked seeds*.

They were the first of all the flowering and seed-bearing plants. They flourished before there were any apple trees or walnuts or melon vines, and have long since disappeared. But their descendants survive in the pines and firs and spruces, the bald cypresses, the cedars and the yews.

Their seeds have little or no protection, although a few species approach the berry-forming stage. The eastern red cedar covers its seeds with white powder, which is food for the cedar waxwing and other birds. The Pacific yew produces crude drupes that birds also eat. The Utah juniper has larger drupes, perhaps a third of an inch long, which hold one, rarely two, seeds. In spite of their piney taste, these seeds were baked into cakes by the Indians.

So-called naked seeds are commonly carried in cones, and the trees that bear them are called conifers.

In some conifers the blossom is cone-shaped. The pollinated buds grow into large seed cones. But the cone is not really a blossom or a fruit. It is a collection of barklike sections which provide some shelter, but no proper covering, for the seeds within. Cones differ greatly in size. We might expect the giant sequoias, largest of living trees, to have the largest cones. But they do not. Their cones are usually about two inches long.

Cedar waxwings feast on seeds of the eastern red cedar.

Largest of all are the cones of the sugar pine which may be twenty-one inches long and more than three inches in diameter. Among the smallest cones are those of the northern white cedar. These are barely half an inch in length, while those of the eastern hemlock are even smaller.

In some conifers the seeds are winged somewhat like those of the elm or maple. Seeds of the white pine have been carried by the winds a quarter of a mile. The sugar pine throws open its huge cones to let out seeds attached to wings that may be five inches long. Each also carries an edible kernel about as large as a grain of corn. Some other pines produce similar kernels called pine nuts. In Siberia these nuts have been an important article of commerce.

The piñon pine of our own Southwest and Mexico may produce as many as eight bushels of cones in one season. The edible kernels inside provided food for the Indians as well as the first white explorers.

Pine cones may need several seasons to mature. Then they expand, and the seeds fall to the ground or flutter away in the wind. In time, cones break to pieces. But those of the black spruce have been known to remain intact for thirty years.

Blossoms of naked seed plants are small. Yellow, red, purple, and even green are common colors. In the Atlantic white cedar the female blossoms, barely an eighth of an inch in diameter, are liver colored; male blossoms are dark brown merging into black.

Millions of years ago, in what is sometimes called the Coal Age, the world was moister than now. Some of our

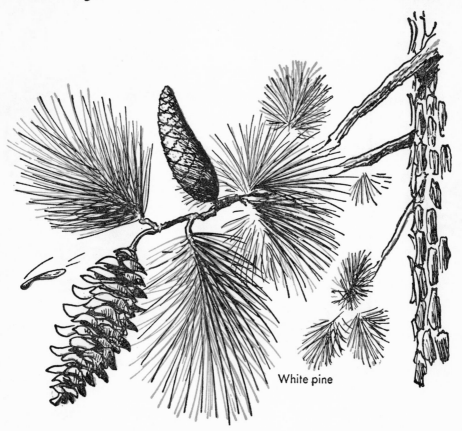

White pine

Little winged seeds shoot out of the barklike pine cone.

mountain ranges had not yet risen to shut off breezes from the sea where clouds are born. In this damp, steamy air naked seeds developed plants of large size. Largest of all, the giant sequoias, once flourished around the world although now they are found only in a few sheltered spots in California. Cedars and bald cypresses also grew to a great size at that time. One bald cypress in Mexico has a trunk more than 115 feet in circumference and is thought to be five thousand years old.

But in spite of their early start, there are only about five hundred species of naked-seed plants today. Although plants from covered seeds made a late start, they soon became far more numerous. For they followed many lines of growth and now number more than 150,000 species.

4.

Plants at Work

Shrubs, Vines and Herbs

Naked seeds developed into trees. And so did some covered seeds. Among them are oaks and elms, beeches and maples, fruit trees and others prized for shade or ornament. But unlike naked seeds, the covered seeds multiplied in other directions.

For they also developed shrubs and bushes. These, like the trees, have woody stems but are smaller. Many like lilacs and azaleas are beautiful when they bloom

The stem of the wisteria may be as thick as a tree trunk.

in the spring. Many others produce delicious berries and small fruits.

Covered seeds also developed vines. Their stems are too weak to stand alone so they trail along the ground or cling to trees or walls. The flame vine with its trumpet-shaped blossoms brightens many a Florida courtyard. The bougainvillea, though native to South America, is a worldwide favorite. In Japan the wisteria with its clusters of blue flowers is considered almost sacred. Even vines without brilliant blossoms, such as ivy, are often beautiful. And the grape vine produces delicious fruit in many parts of the world.

Naked seeds never produced herbs. And herbs are far the most numerous of flowering plants. Unlike shrubs, they do not have woody stems and are shorter lived. Many live only one season and are called *annuals*. Those that survive two seasons are called *biennials*, while those that live longer are *perennials*. Most plants, both wild and cultivated, are herbs. For though herbs are smaller

Many of our most familiar flowers are known as herbs.

and live a shorter time than trees and shrubs and many vines, they are the crowning achievement of the flowering world. They are found almost everywhere that plants can grow. They cling to mountain cliffs and hide in swamps. They add color to the desert and brighten the gloomy jungle. They are the most useful of plants, for they are our chief food producers. And although there are so many herbs, new species or varieties are continually springing up everywhere.

The Leaf and Its Wonders

The flowering plant has three organs: leaves, stem and roots. Flowers, as we have seen, are only modified leaves. Sometimes the process is even reversed. In a field of goldenrod or black-eyed Susans, we may find clusters of tiny leaves that began to take shape as blossoms, then changed back to leaves again.

Botanists recognize three kinds of leaves: *blossom* leaves that become flowers, *protective* leaves such as some palms grow, and *foliage* leaves.

Flowers bloom to produce seed, but foliage leaves have broader tasks. For they feed not only the blossom and the plant that bears it, but all the world besides.

There are many kinds of foliage leaves. Some, such

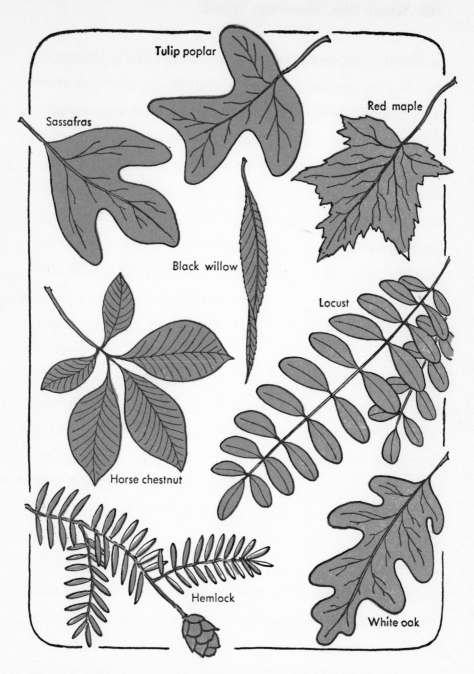

Tulip poplar

Sassafras

Red maple

Black willow

Locust

Horse chestnut

Hemlock

White oak

Leaves are of many shapes, sizes and kinds.

as the lily pad, are nearly round. Others are oval-shaped like the beech. Some are long and slender like the willow, others irregular in outline like the oak or maple. They may have smooth edges or be serrated like a saw. Most leaves are single like the apple or the birch. Others, like the locust or ash, are compound with several leaves clinging to a central stem. They all belong to what botanists call broad-leaved plants.

The leaves of conifers are called *needles*. They are arranged in neat bundles. In the longleaf pine they may be eighteen inches long; in the balsam fir they are short and stubby.

Leaves vary greatly in size. Some are so tiny they look like lace. Yet a leaf of the royal palm may weigh ten pounds. And there are palms in the forests of the Amazon with leaves forty feet long. A good-sized poplar may have 70,000 leaves, a birch 200,000, an old oak 700,000. As for needles, a Monterey pine may have 8,000,000.

Much as "broad leaves" differ, they have a great deal in common. From a central stem veins branch out toward the edges. They provide a framework to support the leaf and also channels for the fluids which feed it.

A leaf seems like a simple thing. But if we look inside

Water comes from the roots to the stem of the leaf.

we find a marvelous laboratory where work is being done that no scientist can equal.

First of all, the leaf has a thin covering that acts somewhat like the human skin. On the underside, in particular, are tiny pores, called *stomata*, that may number 100,000 to a square inch of surface. Each pore has a guard cell which regulates the opening. Some leaves are further protected by tiny hairs as on the woolly leaf of the mullein. Others are protected with scales, still others with a waxy coating.

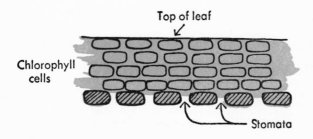

Top of leaf

Chlorophyll cells

Stomata

With a microscope you can see the cells of a leaf.

Through the stomata, leaves breathe in air. So they have been called the lungs of the plant. This process is known as *respiration*. Stomata also give off excess moisture that the roots have absorbed from the soil. A large corn plant may give off thirty-two quarts of water in a week, a big oak twenty-five tons in a month. This process is called *transpiration*.

To breathe in air and give off moisture would seem work enough for things so frail, but leaves do even more wonderful things.

Why Leaves Are Green

Each leaf has many cells. They are so small that only with a microscope can they be seen as separate units. Yet they may contain still smaller bundles of a mysterious thing called *chlorophyll*, which gives the leaf its green color.

Chlorophyll has been called the most wonderful substance in the world, because it can combine lifeless elements into food. It does this by tearing apart their very atoms and rearranging them as we would fit together the pieces of a jigsaw puzzle.

Carbon is the basic element of life. The atmosphere

contains a mere trace of it in a gas called carbon dioxide. In this gas one atom of carbon combines with two atoms of oxygen.

As the leaf takes in air through its stomata, it sifts out the carbon dioxide. This it mixes with water sent upward from the roots. In water two atoms of hydrogen combine with one atom of oxygen. The chlorophyll selects the required atoms of carbon and hydrogen and oxygen from the gas and water, then rearranges them to produce sugar, the simplest of all foods.

There are only three parts of carbon dioxide in ten thousand parts of air. So to make one pound of sugar the leaf must breath in 300,000 gallons of air.

Inside the leaf each bundle of chlorophyll acts like a tiny dynamo. The warm rays of the sun provide the energy. But here again the leaf sifts out only those rays it needs, just as it sifts carbon dioxide from the air. For in manufacturing sugar it uses little more than one-hundredth of the sunlight it receives.

Chemists can tear apart and rearrange atoms. But the process requires a great deal of heat. Yet in its laboratory the leaf uses little heat.

The leaf is also a factory in which more complicated foods are made. For having made sugar from the elements, the leaf takes apart its atoms and combines them with others in more complicated foods such as starch, protein, oil and fat. These are stored within the plant to become a part of the root, stem, leaf, flower and seed.

Leaves not only nourish the plant but all other life besides. Many animals feed upon vegetation. Other animals, the meat eaters, feed upon them. Man feeds upon them all. We, too, can live only because of that remarkable substance called chlorophyll which makes leaves green.

Food and Strength From Underground

Nearly as wonderful as the leaves, are the roots. They provide support for the plant. From the soil they absorb water for the plant cells. The leaves also need water to manufacture sugar and other foods.

Some flowering plants have no root supports. Called air plants, they get moisture from the atmosphere. In the tropics air plants hanging from trees may spread their leaves ten feet or more. Some plants float upon the surface of the water. But most plants bury their roots in the earth.

We seldom appreciate roots because they work unseen. A hickory tree sends down a main central root called a taproot. Willow roots may penetrate thirty feet or more. Many shrubs also have taproots. In some trees, like the spruce and hemlock, roots remain near the surface. The giant sequoia has no taproot nor do its roots extend far. That is perhaps one reason why it grows so slowly and lives so long. On the other hand, the roots of a big oak may spread as widely as its branches. They are grounded so firmly that in a gale the trunk may break before the roots give way.

Large roots send out many tiny branches called root hairs. Sometimes they are interwoven almost like coarse cloth. If the root hairs of a big tree could be laid end

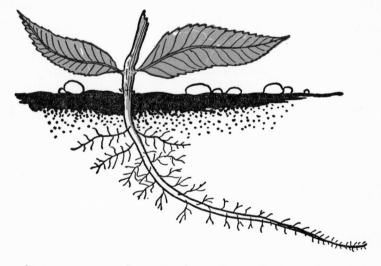

Large roots send out tiny branches called root hairs.

to end, they might measure as much as five hundred miles.

Many smaller plants have long roots, too. Alfalfa roots may go down twenty feet or more. On sandy coasts, beach-grass roots extend even farther. They help to hold the shifting sand dunes in place.

Roots have surprising strength. Groping into a crack, they can split a granite ledge. The roots of a birch, far from the sturdiest of trees, have been known to get under a twenty-ton boulder and actually raise it.

The growing root is tipped with a tiny cap that twists and turns among stones or gravel toward the slightest trace of moisture.

But roots do other remarkable things. They collect not only water but minerals and other substances that plants require. Most important, they collect nitrogen, which is a part of proteins and other complex foods.

Although more than three-quarters of the atmosphere is nitrogen, it does not combine readily with other elements. And so, in spite of all the air the leaves breathe in, this nitrogen does them little good. They have to get help from the roots.

Roots are no better able than leaves to get nitrogen from the air that mingles with the soil. But colonies of

The roots of this tree have split the rock in many bits.

microscopic plants called bacteria form tiny lumps or nodules on the roots. And these bacteria can absorb nitrogen which they share with the roots. Besides, the roots obtain nitrogen from fertilizers.

Most of our foods have some mineral content. When this is lacking, we may suffer from food deficiency. And so may plants. For besides the carbon, oxygen and hydrogen they get from air and water and the nitrogen the roots supply, they may need no fewer than eleven other elements. These are phosphorus, sulfur, calcium, potassium, magnesium, manganese, iron, copper, zinc, boron and molybdenum. Roots seek these elements underground and sometimes collect others, even traces of gold and uranium.

Roots perform another service, too. Although most flowering plants reproduce from seeds, many spring up from roots. When a redwood tree is felled, other red-

The banyan tree sends down roots from its branches.

woods grow about the stump. Trees like the locust and aspen have jointed roots which send up shoots that grow into trees. The banyan tree sends down roots from its branches. These develop new trunks which in turn add others so that a single tree may become a grove. One banyan tree in India has developed over three thousand trunks and given shelter to an army of seven thousand men. Many smaller plants also develop from roots.

Roots may also be storage bins for food. The carrot is such a plant, as are parsnips, beets, and many others. One species of morning glory has roots that may weigh as much as fifty pounds.

Backbone and Pumping Station

The third organ of the flowering plant is the stem. In some it seems more important than leaves or roots. This is true of sugar cane and flax and timber trees. In the giant sequoia both leaves and roots seem unimportant compared with the massive trunk or stem. Yet the sole purpose of the stem is to place leaves and blossoms where they can get the air and sunlight they need.

In open spaces where herbs abound, stems are less necessary. Those of the daisy and goldenrod have only a hard outer layer covering pith inside. Shrubs, however, developed woodier stems. Trees have carried these woody stems even further. For trees had to rise above other plants to reach air and sunlight. They needed sturdy stems to support their branches and foliage.

About three-fifths of wood is cellulose, chemically much like starch. Most of the remainder is a harder substance called *lignin*, which forms the dense heartwood of the tree.

Certain types of wood are very strong. Some of England's cathedrals rest upon wooden piles driven into the ground. We see such piles in wharves and bridges. In Australia wooden timbers have withstood fire better than iron girders. Some trees are well named ironwoods. One tree in South America is even called the "Axe Breaker."

The stem of a plant supports it somewhat as the backbone supports an animal. But the stem does more. Through it liquids collected by the roots circulate upward to the leaves. Such liquid or sap is the life blood of the plant. And the stem acts like an efficient pumping station. Every day through the trunk of a big Douglas fir 300 gallons of water may be raised 200 feet.

In both shrubs and trees stems are usually covered

Liquids are collected by the roots and carried up the stem.

with bark for protection. Even ordinary fires have little effect upon the bark of a great sequoia which may be two feet thick.

In some plants the stem does the work of leaves and even roots. In desert regions most cacti have lost their leaves. What look like leaves are only fleshy swellings in the stem, which also contains chlorophyll and manufactures food. In other plants the stem may perform some duties of the roots. For example, Irish potatoes are not really roots but swollen sections of the stem.

Though vines lack the strength to stand alone, they have developed tough stems. In Africa vines called lianas climb great trees two hundred feet or more seeking air and sunlight. Their blossoms, white with golden centers, are very fragrant. In the jungles of South America, lianas have been found hundreds of feet long. They are so strong that they hold up great trees that have died and would otherwise fall to the ground.

5.

From Our Flowering Factories

Food for All

Long ago, when man was a cave-dweller, he sought food where he could find it. He hunted, fished and robbed birds' nests. He gathered wild berries, fruits and nuts and grubbed for roots. This meant that he was constantly on the move, looking for more and better food. When he learned to plant crops, he had a regular food supply and could settle in one place. He and his neighbors could build homes and cities. And slowly our own wonderful civilization began to take shape.

The green leaf is the factory where food is first manu-factured. We do not eat leaves like deer or cattle, but we find some kinds appealing—lettuce, chard and spinach, for example.

We also eat plant stems such as asparagus and bamboo shoots. Leaf stems, such as celery and rhubarb, are im-portant to us as well as fleshy bulbs like onions and artichokes.

We depend even more upon roots like the sweet potato.

Seed coverings, which botanists call fruits, are even more important. These include many of our vegetables such as cucumbers, squashes and tomatoes.

Shrubs give us blueberries, gooseberries, currants and other seed coverings; vines yield grapes, while from the trees we gather such favorites as pears, peaches and apples.

Quite as important are the seeds. Our grains—such as wheat, oats and rice—are only seeds. So, too, are beans, peas and peanuts. Walnuts and chestnuts and pecans are seeds.

Many oils and fats come from plant seeds—cottonseed oil and coconut oil, for example.

Sweets and Flavorings

Plants not only give us food, but sweeten and flavor it as well. Green leaves create the sugar which forms nectar and yields honey. But many plants also conceal sugar in their stems.

Most important of these is sugar cane. In Cuba and Hawaii raising sugar cane is the chief industry. When ripe, the fields of sugar cane are burned to rid them of leaves and trash. This does not injure the cane which is cut to be crushed in mills where the sap is boiled down to molasses and crystallized into sugar.

In our northeastern states the sugar maple yields a sweet sap in springtime that is boiled down to make maple syrup and maple sugar. In the Far East certain palm trees yield a sap which gives those regions sugar.

Many of our popular drinks are also gifts of the flowering world. Tea is the leaf of an evergreen shrub. Coffee is brewed from the seed of a small fruit somewhat like a cranberry. It grows on lovely little trees with glossy leaves. Most of our coffee is raised in Brazil. There, around the great city of São Paulo, more than four billion coffee trees have been planted.

As the green coffee berry ripens, it turns yellow and then red.

Cacao beans, enclosed in pulpy pods, are the seeds of a small tree that grows in tropical America. They furnish us with cocoa and chocolate.

In South America maté is a favorite drink, brewed like tea from the leaf of a small tree. The cola nut is a seed which flavors Coca Cola.

Plants also appear upon our dinner tables in the form of spices—those strange, pungent flavorings that have sometimes sold for their weight in gold.

Most prized of all spices is pepper. Both white and

black pepper are obtained from the seeds of a vine that grows best in the island of Sumatra. Cloves are dried blossoms that failed to bloom. They are native to the Spice Islands in the East Indies.

Nutmegs are the seeds of a fruit that resembles a peach. These seeds are surrounded by a kind of husk which we use as a spice called mace.

Vanilla is obtained from a seed, and so is mustard.

Leaves also flavor our food—thyme and mint, for example. Even bark and roots are used for seasoning. For cinnamon is the bark of a fragrant shrub native to Ceylon, while ginger is the root of a beautiful flowering plant.

For the Doctor's Kit

Long ago, sailors who explored unknown seas found scurvy a greater peril than storms or savages. And so on land they chewed what they called scurvy grass, for scurvy came from eating too few fruits or green vegetables. Later lime juice proved a better remedy, and the British Navy served it so generously that their sailors were called limeys.

As knowledge increased, many plants proved useful

as medicines. Their healing qualities might lie in the fruits or seeds, the leaves, bark, sap or even roots.

Best known is a small tree that grows on the high slopes of the Andes. Its bark yields quinine, one of the most valued of drugs. The natives found quinine cured malaria, the curse of tropical countries.

The juices of some plants form thick gums much used in medicine. Perhaps the most popular is gum arabic, which is obtained from a small tree that grows in Africa.

For years Chinese doctors have prized ginseng root as a medicine.

Some plants are poisonous, but even these poisons may be useful. The seeds of a fruit grown in India yields strychnine. Though deadly, it benefits heart ailments. So does digitalis, the poisonous juice of the foxglove.

Some plants have the strange power to relieve pain. The juice of the gorgeous poppy forms a black gum called opium. From this gum, morphine is obtained, a dangerous drug, yet one that is extremely useful to relieve pain or induce sleep. The leaves of the coca plant of South America yield cocaine that dentists sometimes use to deaden pain in extracting a tooth.

Opium is made from the Oriental poppy.

Help From Plant Juices

A sweet juice called honeydew oozes from some plant leaves. Ants love it, and bees sometimes make it into honey. In the Near East and in Central Asia this juice is scraped off as sugar. But many plants have juices useful to man.

A milky juice oozes from a dandelion stem. This is so apparent in another plant that it is called milkweed. And a strange tree in South America is known as the cow tree, for natives drink its sap like milk and even use it in a kind of cheese.

Milky juice of the rubber tree drips into a little cup.

Far more valuable is the juice of a plant with glossy green leaves, the rubber tree. The bark is slashed and the milky juice is collected in little cups. It is then dried, treated and made into thousands of rubber products.

A similar tree of Sumatra yields gutta-percha, a milky juice that becomes rubbery when it is boiled. It has been used extensively to cover electric wires and underwater cables. The first Atlantic cable was covered with gutta-percha because it gives fine protection against salt water.

Pine trees have a thick sap which hardens into pitch. In southern states this sap is also collected in little cups. For centuries pitch has been used to make containers waterproof and to keep boats from leaking. Turpentine is obtained from pitch. Another product, resin, appears in varnishes and on linoleum. A finer variety, rosin, is rubbed on violin bows and joins in the music of an orchestra.

More valuable is fossil pitch from pine forests that disappeared long ago. Sometimes these forests were swallowed up by the sea. Along the shores of the Baltic, storm waves wash up fossil pitch which is now called amber. Amber is a semiprecious substance made into many ornaments.

Another valuable plant juice is lacquer. In India tiny

insects suck the sap from certain twigs. This covers them and hardens. Then it is collected, insects and all, and from it chemists obtain shellac. A pound of shellac is the life work of 150,000 insects. In Japan a similar juice is obtained directly from the plant to cover and adorn many different articles.

The sapodilla tree of Central America yields a gummy juice called chicle. Natives, called *chicleros*, hunt for these trees in dense jungles. Slashing the bark, they collect the sap and boil it in three-legged iron pots. After one tapping, a tree is allowed to rest for four or five years.

Anyone who cuts down a sapodilla tree in Guatemala is fined fifty dollars, for chicle is the basis of chewing gum.

Home Sweet Home

Cave men lived when the hairy mammoth and woolly rhinoceros roamed the earth. And caves still shelter people in many backwoods regions. But they are dark and damp and make uncomfortable homes.

Long ago settlers in the valleys of the Nile and the Euphrates learned how to make dwellings of mud bricks. And millions of people in crowded India and elsewhere

Tropical homes are often made of bamboo or palm leaves.

still live in mud huts. But that is because trees are scarce or expensive. For growing plants now provide better homes. Even in cities of stone buildings and big apartment houses most homes are made of wood.

In the tropics, homes are sometimes woven like baskets, from reeds or bamboo, and roofed with palm leaves. In other parts of the world, houses are sometimes roofed with grass called thatch.

Giant logs are floated downriver to be sawed into lumber.

In Colonial times our first homes were made of logs. Then, as men found better tools, they sawed trees into lumber. Now in big mills, saws rigged like chains slice through great logs like butter. Other mills plane rough boards and timbers or turn them into shingles, laths, and many other shapes and sizes. For not only our homes but much of our furniture is made of wood.

Plants for Fuel

When early man wanted to light a fire, he did so by rubbing two sticks rapidly together. Wood was the first fuel and is still an important one. True, we have other fuels now—oil and electricity and still more important, coal. But even coal is a product of flowering plants—the remains of giant horsetails and club mosses and tree ferns that grew abundantly long ago in what we have come to call the Coal Age.

In Ireland and some other countries peat is important fuel. Men dig it in bogs and pile it up to dry. Peat is the fiber of dead plants that lived long ago, or their pollen grains that once collected by the billions.

In some parts of the world wood still provides warmth and even power for industry. Through the endless forests of Siberia it is collected beside the railway tracks to be burned in locomotives. And steamboats that sail the mighty Yukon River use trees along the banks for firewood.

Sometimes men have improved wood for special uses. By heating it in a confined space, they have driven off much of its substance, except carbon. The result is charcoal that gave blacksmiths a hotter flame to fashion wrought iron and to bend horseshoes.

More Than a Grass Skirt

Plants not only give us fire to keep us warm, but clothes as well. In the tropics some natives make clothes of leaves. Grass skirts are still worn in the South Sea Islands. Cloth is also made from the inner bark of the mulberry tree. This is beaten thin with a wooden club over a smooth log. Dyed with the juice of plants, it is called *tapa*.

In our southern states cotton is a major crop. Great regions burst into yellow bloom when the cotton plant blossoms. From its white fibers cloth has been woven for thousands of years. Textiles are important industries in many cities.

Driving through the Dakotas, we see what seem like shallow waters glistening in the sun. But they are only millions of the blue blossoms of the flax plant. When

Fibers of the cotton and flax plants are woven into cloth.

harvested, the stalks are soaked in water to rot the softer tissue. The fibers which are left are then woven into linen.

We get other clothing less directly from plants. In the Orient millions of mulberry trees are grown to feed silkworms which spin soft threads that we weave into cloth. It takes nearly a ton of leaves to make a pound of silk. At one time the export of silk was so important that trade routes through Asia to Europe were called Silk Roads. We might say that they, too, were woven from mulberry leaves.

Now the chemist makes a long list of fabrics direct from plants. He dissolves them in acids, then spins their fibers into threads. Among these are rayon, nylon and dacron. Indirectly they, too, are gifts of the flowering world.

Burlap, Rope and Paper

Plants also give us many fibers stronger than those we use in clothing. In the plant they bind together the tissues of leaf and stalk much as the tendons in our bodies connect and strengthen our muscles. Fibers of banana leaves, pineapple, and other plants are also made into cloth quite as beautiful as linen.

A plant called jute grows in the valley of the Ganges. Its fibers are woven into the burlap of sacks which hold grain and other commodities. In flood time on the Mississippi, jute bags are filled with earth and piled along the weakened dykes to keep the swollen waters from overflowing the lowlands.

Still stronger fibers are made from Indian hemp. This is an herb with yellow-green blossoms that grows from four to six feet high. The Greeks and Romans imported hemp which they twisted into rope. The sails of their ships were raised and the masts held in place by ropes made of hemp. Today ropes of hemp are also used in shipping and construction work.

Fibers from the sharp leaves of the sisal plant are used in making rope.

Another plant with very strong fibers is sisal. This is native to Mexico and Central America. Its sharp leaves, which may be five feet long, are usually harvested by machine. The tough skin and softer tissues are removed, and the yellow-white fibers are carefully dried. These fibers are so strong that one of them would cut our fingers if we tried to break it. They are made into binder twine and rope.

Stronger than either hemp or sisal are the fibers of a shrub that flourishes in the Philippines. It belongs to the banana family and is called *abaca*. The reddish white strands are collected from the rotting leaves and dried like hay. Sometimes they, too, are woven into cloth. But more often they are manufactured into twine and rope. This Manila, so called, is the strongest of all ropes, except steel cables.

The coconut palm also produces a fiber known as *coire*. Coire ropes are used in Africa, where at one time Arabs built queer ships called dhows entirely without nails. Their ribs and planks were tied together with coire ropes. In such leaky craft the Arabs sailed for centuries across the treacherous Indian Ocean.

Even vines may serve as ropes. In Colonial days grape vines were often used in this way. In South America vines called *lianas* provide tow ropes to drag boats up-stream through foaming rapids. They are stronger than Manila rope of the same size.

Another curious fiber grows in the sea. Strands a hundred feet long anchor masses of floating seaweed to the bottom. These open up on the surface like great blossoms 50 feet across, called sea-otter cradles. For the sea otter that swims in those cold waters loves to climb upon one of these living rafts for a nap. The anchor strand, though scarcely a quarter of an inch thick, has been used by the Eskimos for fish line.

Most woody plants have useful fibers. And best of all are those which give us paper. Some of our finest paper is made from rags of cotton or linen. They, too, are plant fibers. Coarse paper is also made from sugar cane. But most paper comes from wood dissolved in acid and pressed between great rollers. Whole forests are now grown for pulp to make paper, another gift of the flowering world.

A Bread Basket of Grass

Scientists assure us that grass is our most valuable plant. Not until it appeared upon the earth did insects, birds and animals multiply so greatly. For grass alone gave them the necessary food.

Green leaves, we know, create the food the plant requires. But many leaves are worth little to animals. Pine needles serve the pine, but even goats will not eat them. A few animals are browsers that feed upon foliage of trees and shrubs. Giraffes reach high among the branches. So does an elephant, although he also likes hay. Moose will strip the leaves from a young birch. But grass is the food of grazing animals, the source of our milk and cheese and butter and meat.

The seeds of most flowering plants are also worth little as food. But in some grasses nearly a third of the weight of the plant is seed. And grass seeds are the food of many birds and animals, including ourselves. For our grains—wheat, oats, barley, rice, and others—are among the four thousand species of grass. So is Indian corn that gives us corn bread, feeds pigs and chickens, and fattens steers. And sugar cane is a grass we would surely miss.

Most grasses cling to the ground. But some grow tall like swamp papyrus or elephant grass which is tall enough to conceal an elephant. Largest of all is bamboo

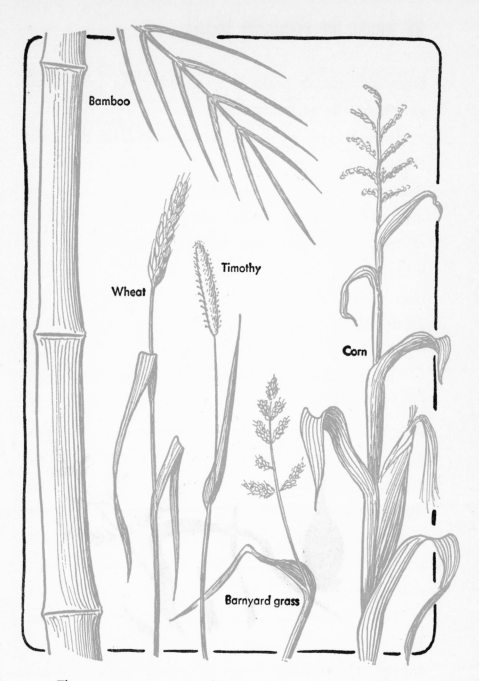

Bamboo

Wheat

Timothy

Corn

Barnyard grass

These grasses provide food for many birds and animals.

which may reach a height of 70 feet. Bamboo has many uses. It is made into fish poles and canes. In the tropics it provides walls and roofs for native dwellings, while joints of the stem make water jugs.

We seldom think of grass as flowering, but it does. Grass leaves grow in opposite rows about the central stem. Among them nestle the blossoms. Usually each bears three stamens, while the single-celled ovary has two styles tipped with stigmas. Few people see them, just as few notice the fainter stars at night. Yet the flowerets of the grass, so small compared with tulips or dahlias, have played a far more important part in life upon the earth.

Enlargement of blossom

Flowers of grass are so small that we seldom see them.

Trees at Work

It is easy for a scientist to name the most important plant. But the most useful tree is a greater puzzle, for most trees are useful.

Among lumbermen pines would hold first place. The white pine is a favorite, for it grows straight and is easily sawed into timber. The Kauri pine of New Zealand has a larger trunk. So has the Douglas fir of our Pacific coast. In Europe the ash is highly thought of, in the Near East the cedar, in India the teak, while ebony and mahogany are popular everywhere.

Among fruit trees the apple is first in the temperate zone. In this country more than 2,000,000 tons of apples are grown annually. But we also grow nearly 5,000,000 tons of oranges.

In cities much thought is given to the selection and care of shade trees. The city of Paris has over 86,000 trees. There the plane tree is the favorite; here, perhaps, the elm. But the red and scarlet oak, the horse chestnut, and others are greatly admired.

Among ornamental trees the copper beech and ornamental maple hold high rank, while the silver spruce adds beauty to many a lawn. Some trees are rated for their blossoms, such as the magnolia and flowering dogwood. Warmer regions have the jacaranda with its blue flowers, the flame red Royal Poinciana, and the gold tree with its yellow blossoms that seem to enclose the very sunbeams.

But the one indispensable tree in regions where it grows is a palm. Unlike other trees palms have no branches. Their leaves are different and much larger. They have no heart wood. They do not record their annual growth in rings like the oak or redwood.

There are more than 3,000 species of palm. Some are small enough to grow in flower pots. The largest of all grows on the slopes of the Andes. Sometimes it is 200 feet tall with a diameter of five feet.

Many palms are ornamental. Others are important food producers, giving us oils and fats and sweets and edible nuts. But two of them stand out above the others.

First is the date palm. Desert peoples in Arabia and the Sahara find it their chief support. They use every particle of leaf and trunk and root. The wood provides timber, the leaves furnish their roofs. From leaves and roots are woven mats and baskets; from the tough fiber, cords and ropes are made. A date palm may live 200 years and reach a height of 100 feet. In good years a

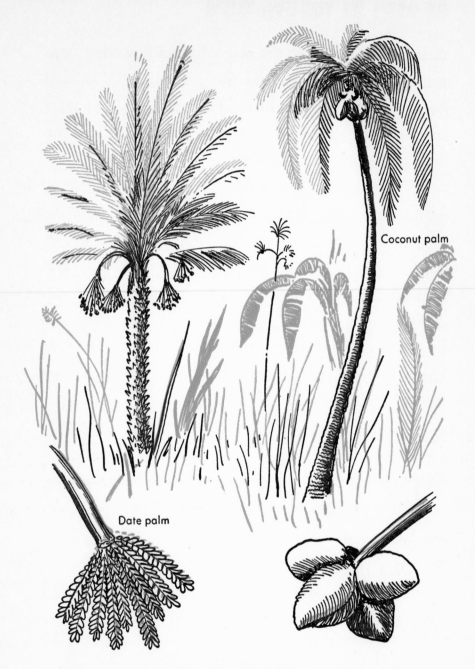

Coconut palm

Date palm

The date palm and coconut palm give us important foods.

single tree may produce 400 pounds of dates, an excellent food. Even the stones, or seeds, are useful when ground into meal to feed camels. A date palm is valuable property, for it may furnish food, clothing and shelter to those who own it.

Just as indispensable and of more world-wide importance is the coconut palm. Natives of coral and volcanic islands have built huts from fallen palm trunks and roofs from palm leaves. From palm fiber they have made fish lines and fish nets. From the trunks they have carved the great double canoes in which they have sailed on voyages of discovery.

Green coconuts contain a sweetish liquid which is a refreshing drink on a hot day. When riper, this turns first to milk, then to white meat. This meat is rich in oil which yields fat for food and oil for lamps and cooking. The empty shells make handy dishes. The bud of the tree forms a delicious salad. The poorer wood provides fuel. More than a thousand uses have been listed for the coconut palm.

In one season a coconut palm may produce a hundred nuts or more. These fall, when ripe, but are better picked before they fall. In some places monkeys have been trained to climb the trees and gather the nuts. But many natives are almost as expert. Placing a cord about the trunk, a man will grasp the ends with both hands and walk upward on his bare feet to where the nuts hang in clusters. But picking them may be unpleasant, for snakes sometimes hide among them or scorpions or wild bees.

The value of the coconut palm is not confined to regions where it grows. The shredded meat is packaged and sold in almost any grocery store. Still more important is the dried meat called copra. In the Philippines great rafts of a million or more coconuts float down the streams to factories where copra is stored. For copra oil is used for many things, the most important being soap.

6.

The Struggle for Survival

Ceaseless Warfare

When grass fails, wild cattle look for fresh pastures. When game is scarce, lions seek new hunting grounds. But most plants, once rooted, cannot move. And so they often struggle for life under unfavorable conditions.

Their greatest need is water. They must have water or die as thirsty travelers have often died in deserts.

Even where rain is abundant there may be long periods of drought. Then wheat turns yellow, corn stalks wither, and farmers fear crop failures. Sheep and cattle starve, and in Russia and China millions of people die from famine.

But too much water may be just as bad. When the Mississippi overflows, not only crops and trees but buildings are swept away. During such a flood the muddy current carries off enough soil every minute to comprise a 40-acre farm.

Frosts are also a threat to plant life. When the temperature falls to freezing in California or Florida, fires are lighted in the vineyards so that smoke clouds may protect the fruit. For not only the crop but the trees themselves may suffer.

Yet, too much heat may be harmful. In mid-summer grass withers and lawns turn brown. Many trees droop as though weary. While plants need sunlight so that their leaves may manufacture food, some cannot endure too much. In coffee plantations loftier shade trees protect the tender coffee bearers.

Plants need air that provides the carbon dioxide for their food. But winds that are too strong may be destructive. When hurricanes came roaring northward some years ago, many a grove of fine sugar maples was uprooted with thousands of acres of forest trees.

When the Pilgrims came, much of our country was forest.

Lightning may blast trees, shearing off branches or splitting the trunks. And it may start dangerous forest fires, although these are more often due to man's own carelessness. In a single year over 200,000 forest fires have raged in this country, destroying fine timber land equal in area to the state of Indiana.

Animals may ruin plants, too. Often goats nibble at young trees before they are well rooted. Elephants ranging a woodland may tear down branches and push over big trees in sport. But of all animals man is most destructive. His homes and cities are built upon land cleared of natural vegetation. When the Pilgrims came

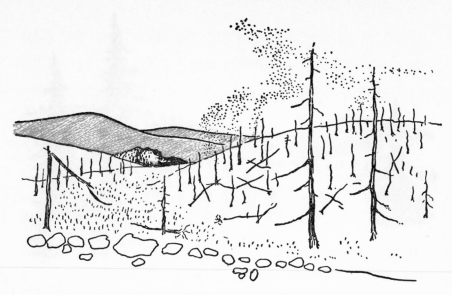

Thousands of acres of forest have been destroyed by fire.

to this country, much of it was forest. Scarcely one-eighth remains untouched while two-thirds of its standing timber has gone.

There is also ceaseless warfare among plants themselves. In one acre of pine woods over 9,000 other shrubs and herbs and trees have been counted. Sometimes such competition is good, for the redwoods of California reach their greatest height when stretching upward above other trees for air and sunlight. But more often it is harmful to plants even of the same species. In a dense growth of pines many are too crowded to grow well.

We can watch this plant warfare in our own back

yards or gardens. Frequently the plants we like must battle others that we call weeds.

In the tropics this struggle may become a deadly duel. There a large tree well-named the strangler fig is a plant assassin. Its seeds, carried by birds, lodge among the branches of a neighboring tree. They send down long roots which reach the earth, then like an octopus wrap around the supporting trunk. More and more the growing fig absorbs water, air, and sunlight until it crushes the very life out of its host. It may reach a great size, perhaps as much as forty feet in circumference. In New Guinea one such "killer" was reported to have wound its roots about its own trunk as if committing suicide.

How Plants Protect Themselves

Many plants have found means to protect themselves. Even lovely roses have thorns. In Africa big game hunters find thorns of the "wait-a-bit" shrubs as effective as barbed wire. The mesquite trees of our Southwest have thorns that will pierce an auto tire. Cowboys in that rough country must wear leather chaps to protect their legs against such thorns.

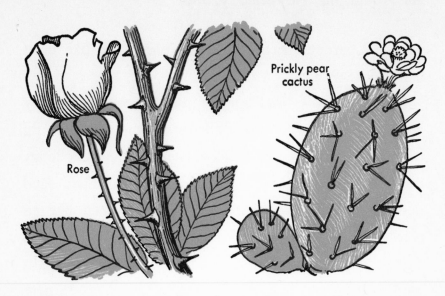

Prickly pear cactus

Rose

Many plants protect themselves by thorns and sharp spines.

Quite as important to plants are smaller spines which are sharp as needles. They cover many a cactus. Other plants are armed with prickles, tiny barbs that pierce and cling. The thistle, national flower of Scotland, though adorned with fringed leaves and beautiful blossoms, is best left alone because of its tiny barbs. Such plants might be called vegetable porcupines because they resemble that curious animal whose quills defend it even from bears and panthers.

Some plants have spines or prickles filled with acid like hypodermic needles. Such are the nettles so irritating to the skin. Australia grows trees whose leaves are covered with spines so painful they drive animals frantic.

Other plants cover their leaves with an oil harmful to touch. Such are poison ivy and poison oak. Species of sumac trees, miscalled poison dogwood, are even worse. Some people contacting them are obliged to go to a hospital for treatment.

Even food plants may have similar bad habits. The mango is a fine fruit, but its skin and even leaves poison some people. Cashew nuts are enclosed in shells just as unpleasant.

Many plants protect themselves in subtler ways. Harmless to touch, they are poisonous when eaten. Animals suffer from such plants. In our northwestern states an herb, known as goat weed, caused heavy losses to ranchers. For sheep and even cattle that fed upon it were poisoned. And the goat weed has many relatives quite as undesirable.

Less dangerous are plants that give off offensive odors. Blossoms sometimes do this to attract flies for pollination. But others are merely defending themselves against birds or animals.

Some plants are even more ingenious. Like actors, they use disguises. Browsing animals have learned to avoid the stinging nettle, with its tiny green blossoms.

The dead nettle is quite a different plant with large white flowers but without nettles. Otherwise, the two are so much alike that only a botanist could tell them apart. Another harmless plant that looks dangerous but isn't is the nettle-leaved bell flower.

One curious plant of arid regions protects itself by hiding. For it looks so much like the pebbles and rock fragments where it grows that hungry sheep and goats do not even see it.

On the Sick List

Plants, like ourselves, have diseases. And since all life depends upon plants, the study of their diseases is important.

In recent years we have learned much about viruses, those strange atoms of life much smaller than bacteria. Sometimes they seem to behave like crystals that form in melted sugar. But unlike crystals, they can reproduce themselves. Perhaps they are the first stirrings of life among particles of lifeless matter. Unfortunately, they do much harm. One destructive plant virus is the so-called mosaic disease of the tobacco field.

Destructive bacteria which attack animals and human

beings are also active in the plant world. But species of fungus do far more damage. They are the rusts and smuts and mildews and blights that can wither growing crops in a single day.

In Ireland, in 1845, a sudden attack of blight ruined the potato crop, the chief food supply. Nearly two million people starved and a million others fled the country. Ireland has never fully recovered.

In our own country beautiful chestnut trees, once common, have almost disappeared. They, too, were destroyed by blight.

Sometimes a fungus has a criminal partner in an insect. The elm-bark beetle is blamed for the death of many a grand old elm. But the beetle only bored holes in the bark which let in the deadly fungus.

While some insects are useful to plants in scattering pollen, some are as dangerous as forest fires. In eastern countries great clouds of locusts sweep on by the billion devouring every green thing. In our western states grasshoppers may be nearly as destructive.

In our southern states the boll weevil, which burrows into cotton buds, destroys, on the average, some half billion dollars' worth of cotton every year.

And there are many other plant enemies. The Hes-

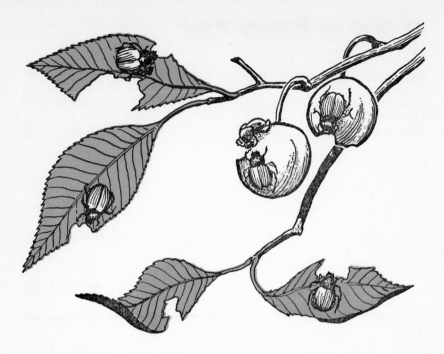

The Japanese beetle is a number one plant killer.

sian fly is a pest in the wheat fields. The corn borer threatens great areas of growing corn. The woolly bug or aphis is a peril to fruit trees and many other plants. The Japanese beetle that came from beyond the Pacific is a number-one plant killer. And the spruce-bud worm has destroyed three-fourths of the spruce and balsam forests of Maine and Minnesota.

Plant Doctors to the Rescue

And so, with all their brave struggle to survive, plants need our help. When we are ailing, a doctor treats us.

All About the Flowering World

Plants also have their doctors—scientists who study their ailments and how to cure them.

Among such doctors are tree surgeons. They examine a shade tree, cut out diseased parts and fill the cavities with cement somewhat as a dentist fills a tooth. They trim branches and paint surfaces where bark has gone. Even trees ready to fall apart are often saved by iron braces which hold spreading branches together.

Fruit trees need continual care. Apple growers wage unending war on coddling moths and other insects that threaten blossoms or fruit. Orange groves and fruit orchards must be sprayed for insect and fungus pests. Cranberry bogs are sometimes sprayed from helicopters. The blight that kills tomatoes, the striped squash beetle and potato bug, the cabbage worm, and many other plant foes must be checked, if we are to have vegetables.

Unseen beneath the ground, other pests may be quite as dangerous. The pineapples of Hawaii were once nearly ruined by worms that ate the roots. Big chemical companies spend large sums in research work trying to find out how to help sick plants to help themselves. And in this country hundreds of millions of dollars are spent every year upon the remedies they offer.

Such money is well invested. For not only our flower

beds and vegetables gardens and fruit trees are threatened but our forests also which provide timber, paper and many other products. It is easy to protect a small garden, but forests are a problem. Lumber companies and paper mills which own large tracts of woodland now spray them from airplanes.

Plants, like ourselves, may suffer from what doctors call malnutrition. Often they do not get enough to eat or fail to get the right foods. Sometimes the soil in which they grow is sour, and lime must be added. Sometimes it lacks some needed element which is added by fertilizers spread on the fields. Where this is not done, the soil is soon worn out and fails to grow good crops. Great areas of this country have been injured by raising tobacco or cotton in the same fields year after year. Now farmers change their crops from year to year or even let the land lie idle for a season or two to rest.

Today many colleges teach farming and forestry, for plant culture grows more difficult, more costly and more important all the time.

Many flowering plants live in swamps and shallows.

7.

Strange Plants in Strange Places

Some Like Their Feet Wet

The first plants that left their home, the sea, flourished in fresh waters. And when many of them migrated to dry land, some still lingered in swamps and shallows. The most beautiful are the water lilies which have great waxy blossoms with golden centers. Their rubbery stems cling lightly to the mud. Although they live amid decaying matter, they create beauty and fragrance. Their leaves, or lily pads, form rafts for frogs or sleepy turtles to sun themselves.

In northern swamps wild moose wade around, munching lily pads. Much other life abounds. Dragonflies flit to and fro, tiny fishes swim about, and water bugs dart here and there where mosquitoes breed.

Water lilies have many colors—creamy white, pink,

yellow and blue. Largest of the family is the Victoria Regis of the tropics. Its blossoms are a foot in diameter. Its pads, sometimes six feet across and curled up around the edges, are strong enough to hold a man!

Water lilies of Africa and Asia are often called lotus. They were sacred to the Egyptians who copied them in the columns which supported their temple roofs.

Water plants often float. A common species is the water hyacinth. Its stems form bladders to support the central stalk of blue blossoms which rises several inches. Great masses of water hyacinths look like meadows in bloom. Islands of these swamp plants drift down the Paraná River, one of the boundaries of Argentina. They carry snakes and larger animals and sometimes nearly fill the harbor of Montevideo before drifting out to sea.

Swamp plants even choke important rivers. The Nile, in its mid course, almost disappears for 500 miles beneath a growth of swamp vegetation. This strange region, called the Sud, is one-third as large as the British Isles. It includes fields of Nile cabbage, papyrus, and ambatch shrubs with yellow blossoms. Elephant grass grows twenty feet high and sword grass cuts like a razor. In places the tangled plants form bridges strong enough to bear up an elephant. Steamboats are sent in to cut out great sections of these tangled plants and drag them downstream to clear the channel.

Water plants also help destroy big lakes. They absorb the water while their dead leaves and roots fill the lake beds with mud.

Many plants love the margins of lakes and streams. Among them are the rushes. They are perennials whose tiny green blossoms are seldom seen. A common kind, the cattail, is a bundle of tufted seeds ready to be scattered by the winds. Important food plants such as water cress and rice also love shallow waters.

Swamp reeds are woven into mats and baskets and even provide walls and roofs for homes. Canoes made of reeds sail over Lake Titicaca, high in the Andes. Reed boats are also common on the rivers of Africa and the Far East.

Some trees love the shallows. Among them are the cypress of the South. Cypress groves provide homes for many birds, water snakes, and sometimes alligators. Mangrove trees even push out into the sea supported on their stilt-like roots.

And so we find in swamps much life both plant and

animal. Many people call them gloomy and unattractive, but George Washington, a surveyor in his youth, thought the Great Dismal Swamp of Virginia and North Carolina "the most beautiful region in the world."

Some Like Them Hot and Dry

Swamp plants have plenty of water and rich soil. Quite different are those in dry or desert regions. Their problem is to survive on poor ground with little water. And through long ages they have solved that problem. For they were the hardiest of the plants which left the sea for new homes on land.

Along the coast, flowering beach peas bloom in shifting sand. And they have neighboring plants quite as beautiful. To live in such unfavorable surroundings many have developed tough stems like the purple sagebrush of the West or the heather that brightens the barren highlands of Scotland. Even ferns, which thrive in the shade and need much moisture, have developed bracken in exposed places.

Amid the bare rocks and hot sands of the desert we find lovely plants. There blooms the desert primrose in colors white, pink and yellow. In arid southwestern states and Mexico the candlewood flaunts its scarlet flowers. There, too, we find the creosote bush with its yellow blooms. The yucca likes dry, open spaces. It belongs to the lily family and because of its sharp leaves is called the Spanish bayonet. The central stalks are covered with blossoms. They are so tough that they are sometimes used for fence posts.

Best known of desert plants are the cacti. Most of the 1700 species are native to our southwest, Mexico and Central America. The cactus makes the most of the little rain that falls in those areas. Its stem is often grooved and covered with sharp spines. These not only keep off hungry animals but prevent loss of moisture. For when showers do fall, the cactus sucks up water like a sponge until the stem swells and the grooves disappear.

Cactus blossoms are among the most gorgeous of flowers. They range from pure white through red, orange and yellow to purple hues. And they are often fragrant.

Many produce edible fruits. Among them are so-called prickly pears. Other species are narcotic or even poisonous. Such are the mescal buttons which Indians chew.

A favorite cactus is the night-blooming cereus. It crawls like a vine along walls or hedges. Its white blossoms open at night to attract moths which scatter pollen. Then, within twenty-four hours, these blossoms close forever.

Largest of the cacti is the saguaro. Because of its queer branches, it is called the candelabra tree. It sometimes grows fifty feet high and weighs five tons. No one knows how long it lives, but it is thought to survive for centuries. A small plant may be thirty years old. When about ten feet high, it bursts into bloom. Its creamy, fragrant blossoms, with golden centers, attract insects. But within a few hours the blossoms close. Their purplish red fruits resemble cucumbers in size and shape. The Indians gathered them by the ton, boiled them to a sweet syrup and used the pulp in jams and preserves.

Quite as tall, though usually unbranched, is the giant torch thistle which may reach a height of nearly sixty feet. It bristles with long spines and bears large cream colored flowers that form crimson, egg-shaped fruits.

Another desert dweller is the Joshua tree. John C. Frémont, the explorer, called it "the most repulsive tree in the vegetable kingdom." Its branches seem twisted as though in pain. Heavy with age, they droop

Saguaro cactus

The saguaro cactus sometimes grows to be fifty feet tall.

to the ground and even fall off. But the tree bears lovely white blossoms tinged with green, and its roots are woven into baskets by the Indians.

Believe-It-or-Not's

Explorers in Sumatran jungles sometimes find the largest of all blossoms. It may weigh 25 pounds and may be three feet or more across. Five thick petals surround the bowl-shaped center, which is large enough to hold six quarts of rain. Flesh tinted or yellow, spotted with purple, they smell like carrion. This attracts swarms of flies which scatter the pollen, for stamens and pistils grow on separate blossoms. There are no leaves or stem or even true roots. For the plant is a parasite that sucks life from some tropic vine or fig tree. The buds, large as cabbages, take a month to mature, but the flower blooms only a day or two. It was named Giant Rafflesia for Sir Stamford Raffles who first described it in 1818.

Many plants do not feed themselves but prey upon others. The best known of these is the mistletoe. One species is not a true parasite, for it has pale green leaves and berries and manufactures some of its own food. But

Krubi

Giant Rafflesia

One blossom of the Giant Rafflesia may weigh 25 pounds. The yellow spike in a krubi blossom may be eight feet tall.

in the South many of these plants growing on a single live oak may kill it. Other mistletoes which are true parasites injure conifers, particularly spruce.

In meadows we find tiny bell-shaped blossoms clinging to the grass. They are dodder plants, with neither leaves nor roots, that send out threadlike filaments.

Where these touch a stem, they wind about it and drain its life. Then, blossoming, they send out other filaments. No wonder farmers call the dodder a pest in pasture lands.

Some flowers are best known for their strange shapes. The bird of paradise flower is like a brightly colored bird. Still more curious is the hand flower of Central America. It has no petals, but from the cup-shaped calyx five red stamens stretch out like claw-tipped fingers.

In the East Indies there grows a huge flower called the giant krubi. From the purple corolla a yellow spike may rise eight feet high. The krubi is sometimes called the largest of blossoms, but it is really a colony that may number thousands. And like the Giant Rafflesia, it has a very bad odor.

At the other extreme are tiny blossoms of the duck weed. They are so small that we can examine them only through a microscope.

One of the most interesting flowers is the orchid. There are two great families, one native to South America, the other to the Far East. Orchids are highly sensitive. They dislike direct sunlight and require a warm temperature. Growers list over 12,000 species with many more varieties.

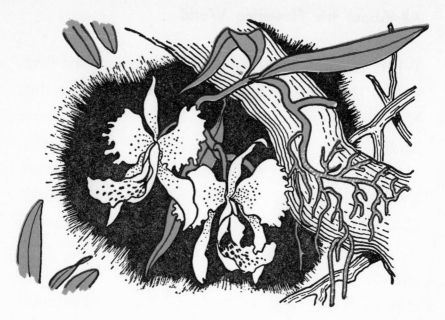

Many orchids are air plants which cling to trees or shrubs.

While few orchids are parasities, most of them are air plants which cling to trees or shrubs. The seeds, fine as dust, may be planted at home. But it may require seven, sometimes even fifteen, years to raise a salable blossom.

Some flowers are prized because they are hard to get. That is why orchid hunters seek rare species in jungles at the risk of fevers, snakes, wild animals and savages.

A favorite flower of mountain climbers is the tiny edelweiss that blooms on lofty cliffs among the Alps. It is the national flower of Switzerland.

Many flowering plants are short-lived. Far different

is the century plant. It belongs to the agaves, a family of over 300 species. Although native to Central and South America, it is found in North America as far east as Maryland. Many century plants blossom repeatedly, but the most famous species may wait fifty years or more. It blooms only once, then dies. For it has completed its life work, the development of seeds.

Many flowering plants are found over wide areas. A few grow only in certain places. One of these is the silver sword. Its pointed leaves, in thick clusters, look as though cut from asbestos. When the plant is about twenty years old, a tall shoot rises ten feet or more from the center. It is covered with blossoms that soon wither. Then the plant itself dies. It grows only in a great crater on the island of Maui in Hawaii. This crater, seven miles long, was called by the natives "The House of the Sun." There, thousands of feet above the sea, the silver sword blossoms in the heart of a dead volcano.

The Insect Eaters

Early explorers in Madagascar brought back weird stories of a man-eating tree. It was said to crush a person in its branches like a giant squid, then drink his blood.

Such tales were false, but there are plants which devour insects quite as eagerly as bats or swallows do.

Among them is the pitcher plant whose vase-shaped leaves hold rain water. It grows in bogs from Labrador to Florida. The leaves are lined with stout hairs pointing downward. Insects, seeking honeydew, crawl into the pitcher. As they do, they fall to the bottom and are drowned. The greedy plant then absorbs their body tissues.

Quite as cruel is the sidesaddle plant. From its leaves hang pouches which also hold rain water. Their rich colors attract insects which enter them and meet the same fate.

Even more treacherous, from the insect's viewpoint, is the bladderwort. It grows beneath the surface of shallow waters. Its roots end in tiny pouches. Curious water insects crawl inside only to be held and digested by the hungry bladderwort which gets its name from the swellings on stem and leaves that float it to the surface at blossoming time.

Different, but quite as effective, is the butterwort of mountain bogs. An insect, lighting upon a leaf, is stuck, as though on flypaper. The leaf edges then curl inward, pushing the insect toward the center where

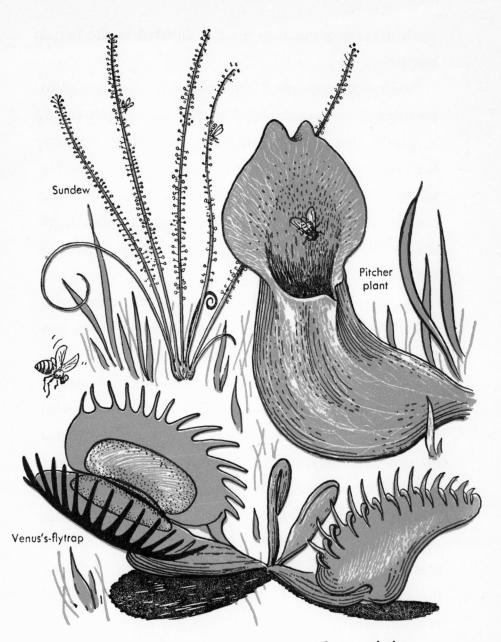

Sundew

Pitcher plant

Venus's-flytrap

Many plants are able to devour insects that touch them.

acids dissolve it much as meat is digested in the human stomach.

Still more ingenious is the sundew, a small bog plant. Its leaves are covered with movable, sticky hairs ending in glands that glisten in the sun. An insect, touching the outer hairs, is thrown toward the center of the leaf where it is held fast. Meanwhile, the leaf pours out acids and digestion begins. Even so powerful an insect as the dragonfly is sometimes captured by the sticky hairs of the sundew.

But the most remarkable of all insect eaters is that called Venus's-flytrap. Unlike the sundew and the butterwort, it has no sticky substance or deadly hairs to hold the insect. Nor does it drown him like the pitcher plant or sidesaddle plant. Instead, it works somewhat like those cruel steel traps rimmed with teeth that hunters sometimes set for bears. About the central stem, which rises a foot or more and carries white blossoms, there is a cluster of leaves. These end in double folds edged with needle-like spines. When an insect touches one of these innocent looking folds, it snaps shut and the spines interlock. Thus caught, the insect is digested at leisure.

All About the Flowering World

Insect-eating plants are found in marshy regions where the soil lacks nitrogen. Because they cannot get this through their roots, as most plants do, they become meat-eaters.

8.

Miracles of the Flowering World

Around the World and Back

Since men first began to raise crops, they have distributed more plants in far-off places than winds and ocean currents have done through millions of years. That story is one of romance and adventure.

Coffee came from Abyssinia. First taken to Arabia, it was carried to other countries. In the West Indies the Dutch and French tried to control the market. They put a death penalty on anyone who was caught smuggling the seeds outside their colonies. But a Brazilian ambassador took the risk, and now most coffee is raised in Brazil where it had never grown before.

Pineapples, which were native to Brazil, are now grown chiefly in Hawaii. Brazil also grew the first rubber trees. But seeds, packed in banana leaves, were shipped to England, then to Malaya where most native rubber is now produced.

Cocoa was first grown in Central America. But now much of it grows on the island of Thome, off Africa, where seeds were taken by Portuguese traders long ago.

The cloves which Columbus was seeking in the Far East are now raised on the island of Zanzibar near Africa. Quinine originated in Peru, but most of it now comes from Java.

There was a time when apples grew only in Russia, north of the Caspian Sea. Now orchards flourish around the world. A strange man once roamed our middle-western states when they were a wilderness. He was so poor he walked barefooted in the snow. But his pockets were filled with apple seeds which he planted along the way. People laughed and called him Johnny Appleseed, but few men have done more to benefit others.

Pears came from the same region that gave us apples. But the first peaches grew in China and probably apricots, as well as the better kinds of plums. China also gave us the first oranges. Seeds were carried by the Arabs to Palestine where fine oranges still grow. The Crusaders, who fought to rescue Jerusalem, took oranges back to western Europe when they returned. Originally lemons came from Burma or northern India. But the grapefruit is related to the pomelo of the East Indies. Pomelos are rather woody and tasteless, but a sea captain named Shaddock took some seeds to the West Indies where they were named for him, Shaddocks. In Jamaica some developed into grapefruit, now common on our breakfast tables. In Florida even cattle eat dried grapefruit peel and lick black molasses made from it.

Our bananas were native to Africa and its coastal islands. Spaniards brought them to America. But other species came from Asia and spread over the islands of the Pacific.

Sugar cane is a product of the Far East and still grows wild in New Guinea. Our most useful vegetable, the potato, first appeared among the Andes Mountains. Now it is a major crop in many countries.

Many a thrilling story could be written of how shade

trees and timber trees have spread around the world. More than a thousand species have been brought to this country. Among them are the horse chestnut, the weeping willow, the Lombardy poplar, cork oaks from Spain, the Cedars of Lebanon, the Tree of Heaven from China. Favorites also are the Australian eucalyptus, the Scotch pine and Norway spruce.

Also there are many trees native to America which have spread to other parts of the world. Our white pine now grows in Europe, our Douglas fir in New Zealand. In 1853 two ounces of sequoia seed were carried across the Great Plains by the Wells Fargo Express, when Indians were still on the warpath. Shipped to England, the seeds took root, then spread to other countries, including India. America also gave the world tobacco, Indian corn and other useful plants.

Flowers, too, have been widely scattered. Our tulips came from Turkey, our hollyhocks from China. Dahlias were native to Mexico, fuchsias to Central America, chrysanthemums to Japan. The Royal Poinciana came from Madagascar.

Better kinds of grain and vegetables are being imported or sent abroad continually. And new types of grass that will live in dry, hot regions are being transplanted to new regions. For everywhere men are trying to enlarge the boundaries of the flowering world and increase the usefulness of its products.

How Men Develop New Species

Men not only distribute plants, they create new species. These appear naturally over long periods of changing climate, soil and moisture. But what might take millions of years, can now be done in a few seasons with the aid of scientists.

This process is called *hybridization*, a long word of simple meaning. Pollen from a male flower, placed on a female blossom of another species, develops a different plant called a hybrid. With care through several generations, a new species may result. In this way men now mold plants almost as a sculptor molds wet clay.

Some years ago Luther Burbank became famous for his work in this field. Among his successes was the development of spineless cactus which cattle could eat. A Russian named Vavilov has cultivated 35,000 strains of wheat. Some ripen in the fall, others in the spring. Many were bred to resist frost or drought, or diseases like rust.

Scientists have developed hybrid corn with bigger cobs and
more kernels.

Such experiments have given us corn with bigger
cobs and more kernels, cotton with longer fiber, tomatoes of better size and flavor. Our strawberries were all
developed from the wild strawberry, sweet and tasty
but tiny. A small variety of watermelon has been developed as more practical for small families and modern
refrigerators.

Our apples show very clearly what men can do by
study and cultivation. The first apple was probably
much like our wild crab apple. But we have improved it
and varied it until we have apples of all sizes, kinds and

colors. Now we have winter apples, cooking apples, cider apples, eating apples. Changes in color gave us the russet, the Greening, Grimes Golden, and many a shade of big red apple. And there are flavors such as we find in the Winesap, McIntosh, and Delicious.

Developing a new species takes thirty to forty years. But once established, it can be registered in the patent office at Washington. By hybridization more than 7,000 varieties of apple have been developed from some inferior fruit in Russia.

We also have 5,000 kinds of pears. In France some species were grown for the royal table. They were delicious and eaten with a spoon. But they were so delicate that they remained at their prime for only thirty minutes. Then they became less appetizing.

We think of oranges, lemons, limes, and grapefruit as four kinds of citrus fruit. But Florida growers list over 140 different varieties. These have been developed by hybridization.

Also many new flowers have been bred for market. Orchid and rose growers spend a lifetime in such experiments. Now we have dozens of different roses, many patented. They are selected for size, color or fragrance.

New sciences are now devoted to plants, their habits

and needs. Studies are made of soil, fertilizer, water supply and sunlight. We have grasses that produce more hay, better yields of grain, and many different fruits and vegetables. And all of them mark triumphs in man's conquest of the flowering world.

No Posies Here

Beyond the borders of the flowering world are those plants which have no flowers. They are refugees from an earlier age. But they were the first to stir in lifeless seas, the first to clothe the naked rocks when the world was young. And they began the grand drama of creation which later flowered in the countless herbs and shrubs and trees we have today.

In the far-off time, the boiling oceans at last grew cool. Slowly the continents rose dripping above the waves. Then, somewhere in sunlit shallows, the right elements combined to form a cell. Most cells are microscopic. They are filled with protoplasm. Unlike grains of sand or drops of water, they have the mysterious power to divide into other cells. And like bricks in a building, they form the roots and leaves and blossoms of plants, the bones and flesh and nerves of animals.

The first plants had only a single cell. They floated or lurked in the mud. They were so tiny we could not have seen them if we had been there. But when they appeared, the world became a different place. At last it was alive.

Just when this happened we do not know. Such plants left only faint traces in fossil-bearing rocks. But scientists have followed those traces back for one billion two hundred million years.

Today we have plants just as small which we call bacteria. They swarm almost everywhere. Most of them are useful, for they help to break up dead matter. A few, the germs of disease, attack living things.

One way bacteria multiply is very simple. The single cell increases in size, then divides to form two other cells. These, in turn, divide. So, impossible as it may seem, one bacterium may produce sixteen million others in a single day.

The earliest plants, however, were probably algae. Many were microscopic. But they contained chlorophyll and could manufacture food. And, unlike bacteria, they finally combined many cells to form a larger plant. Except bacteria, they are the most widely distributed of all plants. There are more than 40,000 species. They

are the vegetation of the oceans. One species floats above
mountain tops and has been found 300 feet beneath the
surface of the sea. There may be twenty-five million
algae in a single ounce of soil. We see larger species in
the green scum on stagnant pools. Algae cling to the
shells of crabs and snails and turtles. They even collect
on the fur of sloths, those stupid creatures that hang
upside down from tropical trees.

The simplest algae divided like the bacteria. The
larger ones developed sex. A male cell swam to meet a
female cell; then both united to form another cell. This
was a spore, the germ of a new life.

For a long, long time plants lived only in the sea.
Then they began invading streams and ponds. But the
landscape remained as barren as the moon. For another
two hundred million years passed before plants ventured
out on land. This should not surprise us, as protoplasm
is nine-tenths water. But gradually such plants as the
mosses and the ferns took root in moist ground.

Now stranger plants appeared—the fungi. They are
very numerous, for some scientists list 100,000 species.
They are the scavengers of the plant world. They have
no chlorophyll and so cannot make their own food. Like
bacteria, they feed upon dead matter. They change the

rotting tree stump to rich soil where violets grow. But some fungi, as we have seen, do a great deal of harm.

Lowest of all are the slime molds. They have no cells but seem to flow over a fallen log and absorb their food. They sometimes grow from spores. They also reproduce by budding. A tiny bud or bunch will form, then break away to produce a new plant.

With the fungi appeared a still stranger plant, the lichen. It is a union of an alga with a fungus. The fungus absorbs moisture, the alga manufactures food. Lichens are flat to get more sunlight, and tough to prevent loss of moisture. Through the years a lichen changes very

Reindeer paw through the snow for the lichen underneath.

slowly. In fifty years it may expand scarcely an inch. Some lichens may be older than oaks. They are the only plant that can crumble a hard rock, for they develop 140 different acids. They also cling to the bark of trees. They are the hardiest of plants. They smear the rocks of Grinnell Land on the frozen Arctic. They are the only vegetation in the whole continent of Antarctica. If some space ship ever reaches Mars, it may find that planet covered with lichens. When our own world grows cold, lichens may be the last life to disappear.

In lichens the fungus may release a spore which will not grow until it meets the right alga. Or a bit of lichen may break away and form a new plant.

Plants first left the waters for dry land three hundred million years ago. At first the fields were green, but there were no flowers. Meanwhile, the mosses and the ferns flourished. Queer plants called horsetails grew 100 feet high with stems three feet thick. Ferns were as large as palm trees. Club mosses reached a height of 100 feet and a diameter of six feet. We find their remains in coal beds, for this was the age when coal was formed. It was also the Age of Dinosaurs and other great and terrible creatures.

In the Age of Dinosaurs plants were very different.

Mosses now cling to many a log or rock. Some are very beautiful. Ferns are a higher form with stems and leaves. Some tree ferns are 60 feet tall. But they are all flowerless plants that come from spores.

It was perhaps two hundred million years ago that plants first developed seeds. A spore is but a single cell, a mere atom of life. A single fungus may send out five billion spores that float like dust in the upper air. A seed is quite different. It has many cells. It is really an unborn but complete little plant. And it is the product of a flower.

For long ages plants produced only naked seeds. We still have them in the conifers and the ginkgo tree of the Orient, that Chinese call the Duckfoot because of its strange leaves. Then, perhaps one hundred million years ago, came the present chapter. At last plants learned to protect their seeds with fruits or berries or nut shells. This was the beginning of the flowering world in which we live.

Next to flowering plants the algae are the most important. Though abundant on land, they flourish best in the ocean. Tiny algae called diatoms may even color the wet sand. In the Arctic they give a gritty feel to the water. Algae might be called the meadows of the sea where fishes feed and even great blue whales. Much larger algae wash up in windrows along the beach or cover the rocks with yellow-green masses. Some species are red, some look like green cellophane. Others, the kelp, have rubbery stalks and leaves. The giant kelp of the Pacific has stalks 200 feet long. Darwin found that groves of giant kelp swarmed with more life than any tropical jungle. Strangest of all seas is the Sargasso that lies in mid-Atlantic between the Azores and Bermuda. It covers an area half as large as the United States. Great masses of floating algae called *Sargassum* are swept there

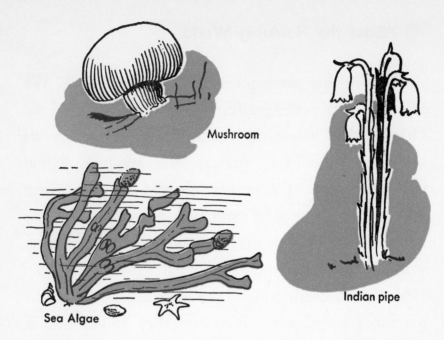

Mushroom

Indian pipe

Sea Algae

Such plants as these are often dull white or colorless.

by ocean currents. Sailors once told weird stories, quite untrue, of ships caught in this sea that could not get out.

Sea algae make good fertilizer. They are a source of valuable chemicals. Several species are chewed or made into puddings. In Japan they are an important food, and even made into candy. Our ice cream is often thickened with a substance obtained from seaweed.

The troublesome fungi do some good. Yeast that raises bread is a fungus, and so are mushrooms. Fungi also give us penicillin that doctors find so useful. Even the lichens have their place. Reindeer paw through snow for the lichen called "reindeer moss." Galápagos turtles, that live longer than any other creature, nibble lichens in their barren islands. And explorers, starving in the Arctic, have kept alive on lichen soup.

Our Best Friends

A great area of our western states is called the Dust Bowl. Once grasses grew there. But after the land was plowed, winds began to sweep away the soil in clouds that darkened the sun. Slowly but steadily the wind carries away the top soil until the country becomes a desert. In this way, soil formed during thousands of years, is lost in weeks or even days.

In other places, where plant life has been disturbed, the rains gouge out gullies, like raw wounds in the bleeding earth. Along the sea coast the winds heap sand dunes like giant snow drifts. They bury trees and even threaten towns. Such places show us all too clearly what happens if we disturb the plant life that protects the land.

Plants also preserve precious water. How moist a woodland seems on a hot day! That is because millions of leaves are giving off surplus moisture. Around large cities, forests conserve the water supply. China was once

In some areas there are few plant roots to hold the soil during heavy rains.

wooded, but as the population increased more land was plowed up for crops and homes. Now over great areas there are few plant roots to hold the soil during heavy rains. Without the roots of trees and sod, rain runs off quickly doing little good to growing crops and flooding the lowlands.

Air conditioning brings comfort to homes and offices. But plants do this on a far grander scale. Because plants absorb and hold the heat, woodlands are always cooler in the summer and warmer in winter than open country.

Plants also purify the air we breathe. Animals give off poisonous carbon dioxide in their breath. But this is just what plants need, for it provides them with carbon.

All About the Flowering World

Every year it has been estimated that plants remove two hundred billion tons of carbon from the atmosphere.

But what is even more important, plants take this carbon and, by combining it with water, manufacture the food which feeds the world.

And so, when we stroll in meadow or woodland to admire the flowering plants, let us also remember in how many ways they serve us. Then we shall recognize them for what they really are—our very best friends.

Index

Index

Index

About the Author of This Book

FERDINAND C. LANE was born in Minnesota, but he has spent most of his life on the East Coast or traveling in other countries. After graduating from Tabor Academy, he studied at Boston University and Massachusetts Institute of Technology.

Throughout a long career of research, writing and editing, he has explored many different areas of natural science. For years he devoted much of his time to study of plant and animal life of the sea. Out of this grew several books including *All About the Sea*.

Although the sea has been his special interest, Dr. Lane has made extensive studies of insects and flowering plants. His field trips have taken him to all parts of the world where he has observed and collected rare specimens.

All About the Flowering World was written while Dr. Lane was wintering in the Hawaiian Islands.

About the Illustrator of This Book

FRANCIS RUSSELL PETERSON is a member of the research staff of the American Museum of Natural History in New York. As soon as he completed the illustrations for *All About the Flowering World*, he left for New Guinea with a scientific expedition to study the flora and fauna of that island.

Mr. Peterson has spent a great deal of time in the field, sketching from life in the United States, Alaska and Hawaii. Much of his work has been exhibited in North and South Carolina where he lived for several years. His illustrations have appeared in *Coronet* and other magazines and books.